CAMPFIRE GHOST STORIES

Jo-Anne Christensen
Illustrations by Arlana Anderson-Hale

GHOST HOUSE

Ghost House Books

The Publisher: Ghost House Books
Distributed by Lone Pine Publishing
10145–81 Avenue
Edmonton AB T6E 1W9
Canada
Website: http://www.ghostbooks.net

National Library of Canada Cataloguing in Publication Data
Christensen, Jo-Anne.
    Campfire ghost stories
    ISBN-13: 978-1-894877-02-2
    ISBN-10: 1-894877-02-0

    I. Title.
PS8555.H6775C35 2002   C813'.54   C2002-910168-9
PR9199.3.C4979C35 2002

Editorial Director: Nancy Foulds
Project Editor: Shelagh Kubish
Editorial: Denise Dykstra, Shelagh Kubish, Chris Wangler
Production Coordinator: Jennifer Fafard
Layout & Production: Jeff Fedorkiw
Cover Design: Elliot Engley

We acknowledge the financial support of the Government of Canada through the Book Publishing Industry Development Program (BPIDP) for our publishing activities.

PC: P5

Dedication

For Vilda Poole,
a good friend and talented
storyteller who never shies
away from the scary stuff…

Contents

Part Three: Stories Told by Candlelight

Acknowledgments

It's time to say "thank you," and it's tough to know where to start. When I am writing a book, I receive help from so many people in so many ways, ranging from contributions as concrete as a story idea to those as intangible as a well-timed word of encouragement. Everyone who is in my life supports my projects in his or her own way, and many deserve special mention.

I am very grateful to the many friendly, enthusiastic people who make up the staff and management of Ghost House Books. I find it difficult to adequately express my deep appreciation for all that you do. In particular, Shelagh Kubish, Arlana Anderson-Hale and Denise Dykstra have made this a better book by lending their tremendous talents to it. And to Nancy Foulds and Shane Kennedy, of Ghost House, I offer my sincere thanks for your continued support.

My appreciation also goes out to Vilda Poole, of Prince Albert, Saskatchewan. Vilda is owed thanks for sharing my stories with so many people over the years in the course of her tireless volunteer reading in the community. I am grateful, also, to Frank Poole— for offering me one of his original campfire stories, upon which I based the tale "The Calling Woman." I also wish to thank W. Ritchie Benedict of Calgary, Alberta, for inspiring me with the many strange stories he sends my way.

As for those who are nearest and dearest—thank you, Barbara, for everything, always. Thank you to my children, Steven, Gracie, William and Natalie. And thank you to my husband, Dennis, who is my constant supporter.

Finally, I would like to express my gratitude to all the great storytellers—friends, family and acquaintances—whom I have ever had the privilege of knowing. I'm sure that most of you aren't even aware of the magic that you create, but if you have a practiced sense of timing, an appreciation for a well-chosen word, and you believe that a single person makes a worthwhile audience, then you have made my world a more colorful and delightful place.

Let's never stop trying to entertain one another with the tales that we tell.

Introduction

We all love a good story—and it would appear as though we always have. Thousands of years ago, people told stories to entertain one another and preserve their history. As society developed, storytellers and troubadours earned an important place among their people and enjoyed the patronage of royalty. Today, stories are as important as ever, although we have moved toward more impersonal forms of communication, such as films and television.

There remains something very special about good, old-fashioned storytelling. It's an experience shared between the teller and the listener, something requiring the kind of quiet and concentration that is rarely expected of us these days. Fortunately, in a world that has become almost too fast-paced to permit that kind of atmosphere, we still have the campfire.

There is something about a dark night and a flickering campfire that urges us to be still and quiet and take simple pleasure in the company of others. It is the perfect place to share a story—particularly a spooky one. There has always been something delicious about sitting close to a crackling fire, with our backs vulnerable to the darkness and the unknown, listening to a well-told tale designed to make our skin crawl, our nerves jump and our flesh creep. Scary stories have become so popular in those circumstances that there are now lots of legends that could easily be considered "campfire classics." Many are ghost stories, although monsters and maniacs have earned a secure place in our lore as well. You'll find many of these well-known themes and legends within the pages of this book.

There are two different ways to enjoy *Campfire Ghost Stories*. The first is to read it to yourself, whenever you're in the mood for that "scary-story-told-around-the-campfire" feeling. The second is to share it with others—around a fire, or in some similarly moody atmosphere—by either reading the stories aloud or retelling them in your own words. This book was written with that sort of activity in mind. Most of the stories can be related in fewer than 10 minutes and many are written in a reader-friendly narrative. All are suitable for creative retelling.

But because we are such a media-fed society, telling a story may not come as naturally to us as it did to our ancestors. While storytelling needn't be complicated or difficult, there are a few basic guidelines to keep in mind, some common-sense suggestions that will make the experience more enjoyable for both the teller and the audience. Tips for telling stories effectively follow on the next few pages.

Ten Tips for Storytellers

1. Select an appropriate story for the audience. The younger your listeners, the shorter and simpler the tale should be. Obviously, very young children don't need to hear anything really frightening, but they often love fairytale-style stories with a few mildly spooky elements.

2. Atmosphere is important. Even if you don't have a campfire, a thunderstorm or a power outage conveniently at hand, you can do some things to enhance the experience. Dim the lights and turn off the telephone. Use candles. Allow sufficient time for the event and insist upon respectful silence from your audience.

3. Be comfortably familiar with your material. Even if you're reading from a book, know the story well. That will allow you to look up frequently to make eye contact with your listeners and will give you more freedom to be expressive and theatrical.

4. Find an exciting way to open the story and capture your listeners' attention.

5. Use your voice, and your body, expressively. Try to incorporate any gestures that might be appropriate and would add a sense of drama.

6. Experiment with timing. The pace at which you read, or speak, should change with the level of action in the story. Varying the speed and tone of your voice will also help you to maintain your listeners' attention.

7. When telling a story, you can create atmosphere through vivid descriptions, but try to avoid being long-winded. It's your job to make the story move; you want to advance the plot at a steady pace.

8. When the story is a scary one, focus on the mystery and suspense, not on the gore and potentially repulsive elements.

9. Don't draw the story out past its natural conclusion. A good story requires a good ending. Also, keeping a strong ending in mind, don't be afraid of the moment of silence that will follow your story. Don't be tempted to fill it with an apologetic "anyway... " or some other chatter. Give your audience time to absorb the story and show their appreciation.

10. Relax. Try to remember that your audience is receptive—they *want* to enjoy what you're about to share with them. It may also help to remember that, even if you're not accustomed to speaking to a group, you probably *are* an experienced storyteller. Pretend that you're talking to a friend and enjoy yourself.

Storytelling is a skill well worth honing—and not only for the sake of entertainment. As I wrote this book, I learned that telling ghost stories around the campfire also serves a wonderfully practical purpose. This information came to me by way of a conversation with one particular gentleman who has made many excursions into the wilderness with youngsters in tow. He was kind enough to tell me one of his secrets.

"Once I've told the kids a good ghost story," he explained in a conspiratorial tone, "I don't have to worry about them wandering away from the campsite. Nobody goes exploring and gets themselves lost. In fact, I practically have to peel 'em off me."

What a perfect reason—as if we ever needed a reason—to enjoy a scary story…

Part One
Stories Told by Firelight

Certain tales are meant to be told late at night, under the stars and in the light of a crackling fire. They are the legends of our time, the urban mythology, or the stories most of us have heard at one time or another.

The teller usually swears that the tale is true, and the listener is willing to believe. That is the magic that is created when there is a story told by firelight…

The Hitchhiker

Donald Whaley was in sales—the kind of sales that required driving all over the countryside, from small town to smaller town, putting many miles on his old sedan with its trunk full of samples and order forms. He did most of his business during the day, talking to housewives, senior citizens and others who were at home and available to hear his spiel about miracle cleaning products. He did most of his driving at night, when people were comfortably settled in front of their televisions and not at all interested in how to get stubborn spots out of their carpets and draperies.

Late one particular night, Donald was traveling along a familiar stretch of winding road that led through a thick forest and into a town on his regular route. As he came around one especially sharp curve, he was forced to bring his foot down hard on the brake pedal. Had he not been alert, he would have run down a young girl who was wandering directly down the middle of the road.

She stood out in the gloom as a vision of pale skin and dripping white silk. In the illumination cast by the headlights of Donald's car, he could see plainly that the girl was drenched. The filmy fabric of her dress clung to her in wet patches, and her long hair was matted into sodden ropes. She hugged herself tightly and shivered in the chill evening air.

Donald held no grudge for having nearly been forced off the road, and, in fact, felt quite sorry for the girl, who was clearly in need of some assistance. He stepped out of the car and called out to her.

"Are you going into town? I'd be happy to give you a lift."

The girl turned around then, and Donald's knees weakened. She was lovely—even with mascara streaked in the hollows under her eyes and her wet hair pasted to her cheeks and forehead. She didn't answer directly, but gave a slight nod and walked toward the car.

Donald ran around to open the passenger-side door, then reached into the car and pulled something from the back seat.

"It's wool," he said as he gallantly placed his own coat around the girl's slender shoulders. "It'll help keep you warm."

"Thank you," the girl whispered to Donald. It was obvious to him that she needed the garment. Her voice was as thin as the watery moonlight, and her waxen skin had felt as cold as ice.

As Donald drove toward town, he tried unsuccessfully to engage his beautiful passenger in conversation. When he asked her how she had come to be soaked, she merely lowered her head and shivered more intensely within the folds of the warm wool coat. When he asked her where she lived, she lifted a hand so thin and pale that it was nearly translucent and waved it weakly in the direction in which they were traveling. Finally, Donald decided that great beauty and the fine art of conversation needn't necessarily be contained within the same package, and he stopped trying to make small talk. The two rode on in silence.

The winding road eventually emerged from the dense, dark woods, and as the car crested a hill, the lights of the small town came into view.

"Now, you'll have to tell me where you want to go," said Donald and, in a manner of speaking, the girl did. With vague gestures, she indicated that he should turn here, or there, until finally they were parked in the long paved drive of a handsome brick home that sat at the farthest point of a dead-end street. The street was poorly lit, but the house was not. Two lanterns blazed brightly by the front door, warm light spilled out of every window, and small bulbs shone along the curved front path, ensuring that no one would stumble over some unseen uneven surface.

"Is this your parents' house?" Donald asked. "It's a great-looking place. A lot of carpets and draperies to clean, though—maybe I should give you my card…"

It was then that Donald glanced to his right and was shocked into forgetting about his business cards and his sample case, and even his stupidly hanging jaw. For he found that he was talking to himself—the beautiful girl was gone.

Donald spun around and searched the back seat. It was empty. Donald was impossibly alone. There had been no sound of the car's passenger door opening and closing, no moment when the girl could have slipped quietly away.

Suddenly, Donald's mind was reeling and his breath felt unfamiliar and heavy in his chest. He loosened his collar with one hand and leaned on the car's worn seat for support.

On that seat, his fingers found an icy wet patch of upholstery. Donald recoiled instantly from the numbing cold. Just as instantly, he knew that the girl truly had been there after all. Somehow, she had snuck out of the car and, he had to assume, run into the house. Of course, there was only one way to know for sure.

Donald walked up the path to the front door and pushed the button beside the name plate with its scripted gold letters spelling "Landon." The sound of the bell had not even begun to fade away when the heavy mahogany door swung open, and Donald found himself face to face with a somber-looking elderly woman.

"I'm not sure exactly what I want to ask you," Donald began.

"That's alright," the woman said. She nodded knowingly and gestured for Donald to come inside. "I expect you were bringing Susan home."

Donald said that although he hadn't known her

name, he had delivered a young lady to the end of the drive, and went on to tell the woman his strange story.

"I don't know how she got out of the car," he eventually concluded, "but she seemed real upset, and I wanted to make sure that she got in the house safely."

The woman shook her head sadly, and Donald noted that she seemed to be aged as much by sadness as by the lines that etched her face.

"No, I'm sorry to say that Susan has never managed to return home, although she tries every year, on this night."

When Donald looked confused, the old woman explained: "It's been nearly 20 years, you see. Since the accident. Susan was at a dance, out at a country hall. On the way home, the car she was in—it left the road and plunged into a lake. Her friends escaped, but Susan was trapped. Every year since then, on the anniversary of her death, she still tries to come back home."

"And this is the anniversary?" Donald whispered.

The woman nodded.

"So all the lights are on because—you've been expecting her?" he asked.

"In a way," the woman answered mournfully. "I've come to expect someone at the door on this night every year. This year it was you."

She showed Donald out then, past a row of family photographs that hung in the broad entrance hall. It would have been impossible for him to not notice one particular framed portrait that featured a beautiful young woman in a dress of snowy silk and lace.

Susan's mother, obviously conditioned by years of the same exclamations and questions, answered Donald before he even had a chance to ask.

"Yes," she said, "that was the dress she wore to the dance, on the night that she died."

Donald Whaley was accustomed to lumpy hotel mattresses and usually slept well wherever he lay his body down. That night, however, he could not close his eyes without seeing the girl's pale skin and hollow, frightened eyes, and no matter how tightly he clutched the rough blankets around him, he found himself shivering at the thought of being swallowed by freezing black water.

But by the time the first thin morning light began to show itself in the gap where the hotel room's ill-fitting curtains should have met, Donald had eased back into comfortable denial.

"It can't be true," he told himself as he showered, shaved and dressed. "It's too farfetched to be true."

But instead of starting his sales route immediately after his customary coffee and eggs, he drove back out to the place where he had first found the girl. He was certain that he would find some clue, some evidence that would calm his mind.

Donald knew the road well and found the hairpin turn easily. It was a short distance south of town, by the narrow entrance to the little cemetery.

The cemetery.

It was a fact that had escaped Donald's attention the night before. That was just as well, for it chilled him thoroughly by the light of day.

It's a coincidence, he told himself, *a coincidence.* Still, he felt drawn into the small burial ground to peruse the grave markers.

The elderly woman had said that her daughter's first name was Susan. The name plate by the doorbell had read Landon. So when Donald found that particular name on the headstone of a well-tended grave, he had to admit that it belonged to his elusive passenger. But even if there had been no name carved there, even if the granite had been smooth, blank and anonymous, he would have known.

For there, draped across the stone, still smelling faintly of lake water, was Donald Whaley's woolen coat.

The Hook

A couple who had just been out on a most enjoyable date were on their way home. The young man thought that his prospects for romance were good and he was reluctant to call an end to the evening, so he took a detour. Soon the girl noticed that they were driving down a dark, deserted stretch of road that was known as Lover's Lane.

"I don't know if this is such a good idea," she told her date.

"Nonsense," he said. "I only want to spend a little more time with you. It's beautiful here, and private. I thought we could get to know each other better."

And so he parked the car in the deepest shadows of the roadside, ostensibly where he and the girl could enjoy gazing out at the moon and stars that peeked through the heavy canopy of leaves. But, in fact, he only seemed to be interested in the view within the car. He slid across the front seat and embraced his date.

She allowed him to kiss her once or twice, but she kept her eyes open. She seemed skittish and distracted, and was more concerned with nervously surveying the area around the car than with pleasing her date. Eventually, he could not hide his frustration.

"What's wrong?" he complained as he pulled away with a pout on his face. "You liked me well enough back at the movie theater."

"I do like you," the girl insisted. "I'm just frightened out here in the middle of nowhere. I heard today on the radio that there's a deranged killer on the loose."

The young man had heard the report too. The murderous maniac was from a nearby asylum and was known best for his grisly weapon—the sharpened metal hook that he wore in place of his missing right hand.

"Alright," the fellow said gallantly. "Now I understand. But there's really nothing to worry about. That lunatic is probably miles from here by now. And besides, I'm here to protect you."

With that, the young man advanced upon his date again, wrapping her tightly in his arms and breathing heavily into her ear. For a few minutes, the girl tried to get into the spirit of things. Still, every snap of a twig or sigh of the breeze caused her to jump and shiver with fear.

When she gasped "What's that!?" for the fifth time, the young man ran out of patience.

"It's nothing!" he snapped. "There is no one here but us! When will you stop behaving like some frightened child?"

His harsh words sent the girl into a fit of tears.

"Well, I am frightened!" she sobbed. "It's so dark here, and so far from town, and I just can't shake this horrible feeling that something bad is about to happen!"

"Something bad has already happened," the young man seethed. "You've ruined our evening. We might as well just go home."

He started the car, threw the transmission into gear and stepped on the gas pedal. The tires spun for a second, then gripped, sending out a spray of dirt and gravel. The car bounced violently as it left the seclusion of the parking spot and climbed up onto the shoulder of the road.

On the drive home, both the young man and young woman were silent. He drove aggressively, demonstrating his fury over being rebuffed in such a childish way. She sat as far away from him as was possible, partly out of embarrassment. She felt relieved that they were approaching the lights and safety of civilization but also foolish for having spoiled the night and invoked her date's wrath over something as silly and insubstantial as intuition.

By the time the young man slowed the car to a stop in front of the girl's house, he had decided upon a suitable plan of behavior.

Even though I have every right to be angry, I'll still get out and open the door for her, he thought. *That'll show her that I'm a gentleman, and then she'll feel silly for having acted the way she did and all the more sorry for having driven me away.*

Without a word, he got out and walked around the front of the car. The girl remained in her seat, feeling sheepish and wondering what sort of conciliatory approach might be most effective. She was lost in her thoughts, but eventually realized that it had been several seconds since her date had left the car, and still he had not opened her door.

She turned and looked out her side window. The young man was there, standing several feet away, looking pale and shaken. His face was twisted into an expression of revulsion and horror. His gaze was fixed upon the passenger door of the car.

"What's wrong? What is it?" the girl cried, and she opened the door and leapt out of the car. This jolted her date out of his frozen state.

"Don't look," he begged her. "Let's go to the house. Don't look."

But the girl couldn't stop herself. She turned in the direction of her boyfriend's gaze and fell to the ground in a dead faint.

For there, hanging from the handle of the passenger-side door, was a gleaming metal hook.

Children of the Tracks

At the edge of a town not far away, there is a set of train tracks that cuts through tall weeds and across a few worn streets, dividing the less desirable part of town into neighborhoods that most would classify as shabby and shabbier. Many of the homes there are little more than shacks; many of the people there are trapped in a cycle of poverty that will never release them. Often their stories are sad, and sometimes they have been tragic. On one crisp fall evening, a young man named Paul drove three of his friends out to those tracks, to tell them one of the more tragic tales.

"Couldn't you have told us at the coffee shop?" complained his girlfriend. The car's heater was broken and there was a good movie playing at the fourplex in the mall. It seemed to her that sitting in discomfort, listening to one of Paul's farfetched tales was a waste of an evening.

"It wouldn't have been the same, telling the story somewhere else," Paul explained. "You wouldn't have believed me."

"Like this will make a difference," said one of the friends in the back seat.

Paul ignored the comment and made a right-hand turn onto the shadowy street that crossed the tracks. The pavement rose up in a little hill to meet the rail bed, and when the car reached the plateau that lay directly across the rails, Paul slowed it to a stop. The car was straddling the tracks.

Paul's friends were about to voice their objections when he distracted them by doing something even more curious. He stepped out of the car, went around to the back and pulled a small sack of white flour out of the trunk. He ripped the bag open and sprinkled its contents liberally over the chrome bumper. Paul's friends watched through the rear window with expressions of blank confusion.

When Paul climbed back into the car, all three of his passengers asked for an explanation.

"I'll tell you later," was all he said. "It'll make sense to you then."

And then he turned to them and told his story.

"Not so long ago," he began, "there was a poor family who lived down there, at the end of that street. There were seven of them, in a little shack of a house. Five kids. One day, the father piled all of those kids into the back of his old, beat-up pickup truck, because they were going across town to visit their grandmother. They got as far as the train crossing—right here, where we are now—when the truck stalled. It wasn't in the best of shape, and it often did that. Usually, the father knew how to fiddle with the engine to get it started again. But on this particular night there was no time to turn the ignition key just so or to feather the gas pedal. On this night, he had crossed the tracks at a bad time and misjudged the distance of the massive train that was rolling toward them.

"He jumped out of the cab, but before he could do anything to save the kids, who were bundled up in the box of the truck and too stunned to move, the train was on them. The wreck was terrible. They say that people heard the sound of twisting metal for miles. The children, though, they didn't make a sound. Didn't have time. And they died, all five of them."

Paul's girlfriend shivered in her fake fur jacket.

"That's depressing," she declared. "Did you haul us all the way out here just to depress us?"

"No, there's more," Paul told her. He allowed a moment's silence for dramatic effect and then carried on.

"A few months after the accident happened, a woman was driving over the tracks, here, when she ran out of gas. Her car gave out, right on the rail bed. Right where all those little kids had died. That alone probably gave her the chills. But the fact that there was a train chugging down the track toward her, that definitely would have done it.

"She was just about to abandon her car when, suddenly, it started to roll. It rolled right off the tracks, here, and down that little slope, and stopped at the bottom. The train roared by, and her car wasn't so much as scratched."

"So the car rolled down the hill. Big deal." One of the fellows in the back seat found it difficult to mask his boredom.

"But the track bed isn't on a slope," Paul countered. "And anyway, that wasn't the only time that happened. About a year after that, someone had a tire blow out, right on this spot, and the rim wouldn't roll over the rail. Again, there was a train coming. And again, in the nick of time, the car mysteriously moved out of harm's way. It's happened plenty more times since then. And everybody around here thinks the same thing: those people were saved by the spirits of those little kids who died when the train hit them.

"Think about it," Paul said, and his eyes were shining with wonder, "the ghosts of five little kids who don't want anyone else to meet the same fate!"

Paul's girlfriend cleared her throat, and the two youths in the backseat snorted derisively.

"Yeah, whatever," said one of them. "But if you don't mind, I'd like to get back to civilization."

"Me, too," said the other. "Plus, if you don't move this heap, we'll be the next ghosts haunting the track. The 8:15 train is comin' through here any time."

Right on cue, a whistle sounded in the distance. All four people in the car turned to look in the direction of the sound, and Paul's girlfriend plucked nervously at his sleeve.

"Let's go," she pleaded.

Paul looked at her and smiled slyly.

"No," he said, and his voice was smooth and confident. "Let's stay. Let's stay and see what happens."

And with that, he reached forward and switched off the car's ignition.

The boys in the backseat wasted no time on tact.

"You're nuts," announced one.

"Totally," agreed the other. And with the sound of simultaneously slamming doors, they were gone.

Paul's girlfriend was less willing to be seen as a deserter. She appealed to Paul one more time.

"Please, the train's getting close!"

She was right. The engine was visible in the distance. Its headlight shone on half of Paul's grinning face, giving him a maniacal appearance. When he made no response and no move to start the car, his girlfriend reached for the keys.

Paul was faster. He snatched the keys out of the ignition and threw them out his half-open window into the tall grass that grew between the tracks and the street. It was more than his girlfriend could stand, and she fled the car screaming.

"You're crazy, Paul!" she shrieked. "You're going to die!" The approaching train underscored her prediction with a prolonged blast of its whistle. Paul paid no attention to the warning, though. He simply sat in the car, his face calm but his eyes bright with excitement as he watched untold tons of steel bearing down on him.

The few seconds that followed were chaos. The intense white headlight of the train became blindingly bright as it drew closer. The blaring of its whistle mixed with the grinding sound of brakes being applied and the frantic sideline shouts of Paul's horrified companions. Only Paul remained still, quiet and expectant as he sat behind the wheel.

His expectations were rewarded when he felt the car shudder. It began to rock a little, then rolled forward, slowly but steadily. The vehicle cleared the track bed and began to roll down the short incline no more than a half second before the train thundered past.·

The car came to a stop and Paul leapt out with his hands raised triumphantly in the air. His girlfriend ran to him, sobbing. His friends approached more slowly. They were relieved, but still angry.

"I told you!" Paul whooped. "You saw it for yourselves! The little ghost kids saved me!"

"Shut up!" one of his friends screamed in response. "You got lucky! It's an optical illusion—those tracks have to be on a hill! You almost got yourself killed telling us a stupid ghost story, and there's no such thing as ghosts!"

"Oh, really?" said Paul, and his voice was, again, like silk. He walked around to the back of the car, and a smug smile spread across his face. Eventually, his friends followed. When they saw what he was looking at, their eyes grew wide and their jaws dropped open in astonishment.

The proof was plain to see. On the chrome bumper, in the heavy dusting of white flour about which they had all forgotten, there they were: five distinct sets of child-sized handprints.

The Warning

A woman who was leaving on a long road trip was planning to drive through the night to a city several hundred miles away. She was traveling alone, which made her mother nervous.

"Be careful," cautioned the mother. "Don't trust strangers. There's a maniac on the loose, you know, and he preys on single young women just like you."

The woman was quick to dismiss her mother's fears. It was true that there was a man who had escaped from a nearby prison, and it was true that he had abducted two young women and brutally murdered them with a large butcher knife, but what of it? The woman felt that there was nothing to be afraid of, as long as a person was street-smart and kept her wits about her.

"Don't worry about me," she told her mother laughingly. "I'll be fine. I know how to take care of myself."

She had meant what she said, but the warning lingered on her mind.

The sun had already set when the woman stopped at a lonely service station by the side of the highway. Heavy clouds obscured the moon and stars, and a rainstorm threatened.

Hurriedly, she filled the gas tank and made use of the dingy little restroom. When she approached the counter to pay her bill, the attendant smiled in a friendly fashion.

"Looks like it's going to be a nasty night," he said as he used a grimy thumb to point at the way his outdoor signs were whipping in the wind.

The young woman nodded but said nothing. In the gloom of night, away from the comforting lights of town, she didn't feel as courageous. The service-station attendant might have been a perfectly fine person, but she had no way of knowing that for certain. He was a stranger to her, and she had been warned to not talk to strangers. As she thought of this, she took her change from the man and hurried out the door, toward the safety of her car.

She was almost there when she heard the bells on the door jangle behind her.

"Wait a minute!" the attendant called after her.

The woman didn't turn. Instead, she quickened her pace.

"I'm in a hurry!" she lied as she ran around the front of her car and yanked open the driver's side door. She slid in behind the wheel, closed the door and locked it. When she looked up, she saw the attendant standing inches away.

Inside the well-lit station, he had appeared to be only a little grubby and disheveled. But outside, under the arc of unnatural fluorescent bulbs, the attendant had taken on a decidedly unsettling countenance.

His face was pale and unshaven, and his eyes were wide and darting. When he spoke, even his voice had a different quality.

"I made a mistake," he said to the woman. "Gave you the wrong change. Just come back inside for a minute and we'll sort it out."

A dense, cold knot formed within the woman's stomach.

"I have to go! I don't care about my change!" she yelled through the closed window. She turned the ignition key and breathed a silent prayer of thanks when her occasionally unreliable car roared to life.

But the attendant was insistent.

"No, it's you who owes me money," he said. "It'll just take a minute. Then you can be on your way!"

He stepped in front of the woman's car then, blocking her way. More than his nervous gaze or his obvious lie, this frightened her. She fumbled in her purse for a handful of coins, and opened her window just wide enough to throw the money out.

"Here!" she cried. "That's more than enough! Now, let me go!"

The attendant leaned forward. He placed his hands on the hood of the car and looked directly into the woman's eyes. Slowly, he shook his head. Silently, he mouthed the word "no."

It was so threatening, so loathsome, the woman was jolted into action. She put the car in gear and stepped on the gas pedal. The attendant jumped out of the way, barely in time. The front fender of the car still managed to brush his thigh with enough force that he was knocked down and sent rolling across the pavement.

As her car swerved wildly onto the highway, the woman risked one backward glance. To her horror, she saw the attendant making a limping run for the pickup truck that sat parked in the stall marked "employees."

She pressed her foot into the gas pedal, pushing the car to its limit. But the car's limit was less than enough, and soon there were headlights looming behind her. In the darkness, the woman couldn't see that it was the attendant's truck following her, but she knew. The driver repeatedly flashed his headlights on high beam and blasted his horn insistently.

Oh my God! the woman thought. *He's trying to drive me off the road!*

The truck advanced until it was scant inches away from the car's bumper, and its horn blared out with deafening persistence. When the driver backed off slightly, it was only so that he could blind the woman with a staccato flashing of lights. Between this terrifying interference and her own state of panic, the woman feared that it wouldn't be long before she misjudged one of the twists and turns of the dark highway.

As she was thinking that, she sped past a familiar sign. "U-Pick Produce, ½ Mile," it read, and the woman remembered the farm where she had once filled a gallon bucket with fresh blueberries. She knew that the drive was coming up on her right; it was a sharp turn that drivers were apt to miss, unless they were prepared…

The woman saw the gravel lane and cranked hard on the steering wheel. She felt the car go up on two tires, where it wobbled briefly before coming down with a spine-compressing thud.

There was noise then, a violent noise that began with a squealing of rubber on pavement, as the pickup truck tried too late to follow the car. The noise was followed by the brittle snapping of tree trunks and the scream of twisting metal. Finally, there was the soft whoosh of flames. The truck had left the road and torn a destructive path down the shallow gully that divided the highway and the U-Pick Produce drive.

The woman felt overwhelming relief wash through her. She slowed the car, turned it around, and with a trembling hand shifted it into park. For a moment, she watched the flaming wreckage that imprisoned the maniacal service-station attendant. Then she closed her eyes, leaned forward until her damp forehead was touching the steering wheel, and waited for the tears to come.

But they didn't. In their place, there was a strange sensation of triumph.

I was right, the woman thought. *I know perfectly well how to take care of myself! There's never a reason to be afraid, as long as I keep my wits about me!*

When she finished congratulating herself, the woman sat up once more and opened her eyes. Some small movement in the rearview mirror captured her attention, and she glanced up to see what it might be.

It took only a split second for her to realize that she had been wrong. Wrong about her cocky beliefs and wrong about the poor, dead service-station attendant. He hadn't been trying to kill her; it was suddenly clear that he'd been trying to warn her.

For there, in the deep shadows of the back seat, sat a large man with a leering eye and an evil smile. When he noticed the woman looking at him, he smiled more broadly and held something up.

The flickering orange flames of the burning truck wreckage reflected so beautifully in the polished razor-edged blade of his very large butcher knife.

Bloody Mary

It was Kelly Parson's 14th birthday, and she was hosting a slumber party in the basement rec room of her parents' home. There were big bowls of popcorn and potato chips, and a greasy box with a couple slices of forgotten pizza sitting on the coffee table. There were endless music videos coming out of the small television set. There were sleeping bags, too—five in total. They were for Kelly, her three best friends and her 11-year-old sister, Carmen. Carmen had been included only because the girls' parents had said there would be no party otherwise.

Kelly and her friends asserted their superiority by making it clear to Carmen that while they could be forced to endure her presence, they could not be made to actually acknowledge it. They gossiped and danced and did each other's hair and makeup, all while managing to exclude the younger girl completely.

Carmen was accustomed to receiving abuse and rejection from her sister. To be ostracized by a group was significantly more demoralizing, though, and she soon decided that she would be better off upstairs, in her own small bedroom.

"Where do you think you're going?" Carmen had only climbed three steps when Kelly grabbed her by the hair and pulled her back down.

"Ow!" complained Carmen. "What do you care if I leave? You don't want me around."

"Truer words were never spoken," lamented Kelly in a world-weary tone. Her friends snickered obediently. "But if you go upstairs with that 'boo-hoo' face, Mom and Dad will think I've been mean to you, and they will come down here and put a damper on our party. Believe me, otherwise I wouldn't care."

"Well, I don't care, either," Carmen said bravely. "And you have been mean to me! You won't let me do anything that you're doing, and you won't talk to me. So I'm going."

Carmen turned and began to march up the stairs.

"Okay, you win," said Kelly.

"What do you mean?" Carmen asked cautiously as she turned around.

"You can hang out with us. Do what we're doing."

Kelly's friends began to moan in objection, but she silenced them with a slight wave of her hand.

"I was thinking," she said in a level voice, "that we could play 'Bloody Mary.' "

There was a moment of complete silence.

Carmen finally said, "What's that?" and there was a snort of laughter from one of Kelly's minions. She was silenced with rapid-fire elbow jabs from the other two.

"It's sort of a game—but a serious one," Kelly explained coolly. "It's not for kids, so if you think you can't handle…"

"I can handle anything you can handle," said Carmen, and she walked back down the stairs. Kelly smiled.

Five minutes later, the television had been turned off, as had the lights. The girls were huddled outside the small basement bathroom. Candles had been lit and placed in front of the vanity mirror, on either side of the sink. In this shadowy, flickering atmosphere, Kelly gave Carmen her instructions.

"It's a great challenge," she told her saucer-eyed sister, "and a dangerous one. You're going to perform a ceremony to summon the spirit of a powerful, long-dead witch. Her name was Mary Worth—but she was known to most as 'Bloody Mary.' Now, what you need to do is stand in front of the mirror and close your eyes. Then spin around 13 times, and each time say 'Bloody Mary.' Say it with feeling, and concentrate on drawing her spirit back from the grave. After the 13th turn, you can open your eyes and look into the mirror. If you see the hag's face, the chant has worked. Then be careful—because she'll try to scratch your eyes out. But if you're strong enough, you can will her to give you her power."

Carmen swallowed hard. She looked into the small bathroom, which with two candles and a story had been transformed into a terrifying altar. Then she looked at Kelly. The older girl nodded, and Carmen knew that she had no choice but to walk through the door. She had to prove herself to the older girls.

The instant that the bathroom door clicked shut, Kelly and her friends let their solemn expressions crumble. They clapped their hands over their mouths to keep hysterical laughter from escaping.

"Shh! Shhhhh!" Kelly hissed. "If she hears you, she'll figure it out! Now, go hide! In a minute, she'll come out of that bathroom all freaked out and dizzy, and we'll take turns jumping out at her! She'll probably pee her pants—which should prove to Mom and Dad that she's too immature to hang out with us."

The girls scattered then and found furniture, walls and draperies to hide behind. They forced themselves to stop snickering, and waited.

Kelly had positioned herself on the far side of an old storage cabinet near the bathroom. With her ear pressed against the wall, she could hear Carmen's voice chanting the witch's name. Silently, Kelly counted along. At the 13th repetition, she felt a wicked little thrill of excitement. She held her breath and prepared to pounce.

For several seconds, there was nothing but silence. Then came a scream that shattered that silence and turned Kelly's excitement to panic.

"Carmen!" Kelly yelled as she ran from her hiding place to the bathroom door. "Knock it off!"

But the screams continued. Kelly tried the doorknob, but found it locked. She pounded on the door with the heel of her hand.

"Get out here, dimwit! Mom and Dad are probably on their way down!"

"Should we stay in our hiding places?" one of the girls asked.

"No, you idiot! Get over here and help me with the door! Turn on some lights! Do something useful!"

Kelly could hear her parents then, scurrying across the creaking hardwood on the main floor. She knew that she had only seconds to get her hysterical sister, and the situation in general, under control.

"I'm coming in, Carmen!" she warned, and threw her shoulder hard against the door. The flimsy lock gave way, and Kelly fell gracelessly on the cold bathroom tile.

The bathroom was in total darkness. The candles had either gone out or been put out, and Kelly found that there wasn't enough light to see her own hand in front of her face, let alone her sister, who was somewhere in the area of the shower stall, if one could judge by where the whimpers and moans were coming from.

"Someone turn on a damn light!" demanded Kelly, and someone did.

Light filled the bathroom and revealed the gory scene that was within it. Slashes of crimson formed a horrifying cross-hatch pattern on the mirror and vanity top. Wet, red handprints smeared the back wall and the opaque glass door to the shower stall.

Using two fingers, as though she was touching some repulsive thing, Kelly pulled open that door. There, crumpled on the floor of the stall, was Carmen. She raised her head, showing Kelly and the others that her face was covered in a network of bleeding lacerations.

"I saw Bloody Mary," she rasped through jaggedly cut lips.

And then it was Kelly's turn to scream.

Six days later, Carmen came home from the hospital. Her face was covered in white patches of dressing, and she was missing a small bit of hair, where one row of stitches extended. Aside from that, she looked fine, almost better than her parents, who wore expressions of great concern and had been told to watch their daughter closely for any signs of self-destructive behavior.

She announced that she was going downstairs to watch television, and after a flurry of persistent, silent gestures from their parents, Kelly said that she would join her.

For a while, the girls watched quietly. Finally, Kelly asked Carmen how she was feeling.

"I feel good," was Carmen's answer. "I feel really, really good. Because, Kel, a few things are going to change around here."

"Right," snorted Kelly. "I doubt it."

Carmen only looked at Kelly and smiled. Behind the bandages and scabs, there was a confidence the girl had never before shown.

"First, I want my CDs back," she said. "And my swim goggles. And the next time your moronic friends want to come over, just tell them 'no.' "

Kelly looked at Carmen and shook her head.

"You really did flip out," she concluded. "You're a nut case, just like I always said."

Carmen barely reacted to her older sister's diagnosis. She turned casually back to the television.

"Nah, I'm not crazy. I'm just different since I saw Bloody Mary. You're going to have to listen to me now."

"You did not see Bloody Mary," Kelly said, although she was regarding Carmen nervously.

"Oh, yes I did," Carmen insisted, and she turned back to face her sister and leaned in close. "I saw Bloody Mary—and she looked just like me."

This time, the girls' parents responded to the screams in half the time. Oddly enough, though, there was twice as much blood.

The Message

A young college student was studying in her dorm room when her roommate walked in.

"I'm exhausted," complained the roommate. "Would you mind studying somewhere else, so I can get some sleep?"

The student was sympathetic and readily agreed. She gathered up her books and her papers and walked across campus to the library.

She had been working there for hours when a group of friends found her. They told her that she looked as though she needed a break and that they were on their way to a pub, which would be just the thing to take her mind off her books.

The student hesitated for only a moment or two. Then she agreed to go, but said that they'd have to stop by her dormitory on the way, so she could pick up her wallet and a sweater. Everyone agreed.

"Wait here," the student said to her friends when they reached the front steps of the building. "I'll only be a minute." She ran lightly up the stairs to her floor and walked softly down the hallway.

When she reached the door to her room, she inserted the key and turned the knob ever so slowly and quietly. She was determined not to disturb her sleeping roommate. With that in mind, she paused when her fingers touched the light switch.

The light will surely wake her, the student thought. *And really, I don't need to turn it on.* After all, the room was very small and she was very familiar with every square inch of it. So she stepped quietly into the darkness and closed the door to the hall behind her.

She took a few steps into the room, with her hands held out cautiously. When her fingers touched the little desk where she did most of her studying, she stopped. She set her books on the desktop, and then, very slowly and quietly, pulled open the top drawer. A few seconds later, she felt the familiar worn leather of her wallet. She picked it up and closed the drawer.

The young student then inched across the room to the one tiny closet the two girls shared. She let her hands lead her along the wall until she came to the closet door. Her roommate had left it ajar, which made it easier to quietly reach inside and grope around until she felt the nubby woolen sleeve of her warmest cardigan. The student slipped the sweater from its hanger, wrapped it around her shoulders and left the room as quietly as she had entered.

The girl rejoined her friends, who had been waiting patiently. The group proceeded to the pub, where they enjoyed themselves completely.

Several hours later, the student finally returned to her dormitory. She was met there by a most disturbing scene. Several police cruisers sat in front of the building, their lights flashing with eerie rhythm.

There was an ambulance, too, and a dark sedan discreetly marked "coroner." Crime scene barricades were being erected on the lawn, which swarmed with uniformed cops and somber-looking detectives.

"What happened here?" the student asked person after person. No one would give her an answer. "Is someone hurt? Who is it?" she begged. "I have to know if my roommate's alright!"

"There'll be a statement issued in the morning," was all anyone would say. But the young student couldn't wait until then to find out if her roommate was safe. She ran into the building and up the staircase, ignoring the barricades and ducking under the lines of yellow crime scene tape. She dodged every person who tried to stop her and ran until she reached the hall outside her door. She was horrified to see a concentration of investigators there.

"Who let this girl in?" barked a red-faced detective who appeared to be in charge.

"Please," the student gasped, "that's my room. I need to find my roommate."

The detective softened a little and walked over to the student's side.

"I'm sorry," he said. "We'll need to talk to you, miss. I'm afraid your roommate is dead. Some maniac murdered her—somewhere around seven o'clock, we think."

The student felt faint.

"That's impossible!" she said. "I stopped back here about seven thirty. Everything was fine."

"You were here, this evening?" asked the detective.

"Yes, for a minute. To get a sweater and my wallet."

"Well, then," the detective said, "perhaps you can help us make sense of something."

He led her into the room then, being careful to shield her eyes from the grisly scene being photographed and investigated. He directed her into the bathroom and flipped on the light switch.

"Do you have any idea what this means?" the detective asked the student. He pointed to the mirror.

The student looked up and felt her knees weaken. Written on the glass, in dried streaks of crimson, was a message. Clearly, it had been left for her.

It read: **Aren't you glad you didn't turn on the lights?**

Skinned Tom

The heavy side door of the honky tonk opened with a rusty groan, spilling a drunken man and woman and a few bars of lively fiddle music out into the humid summer night. It closed with a loud slam, which announced to the couple that they were officially separated from the crowd and the party. They stood alone in the red glare of the exit sign, wondering what to say to one another now that they no longer had to shout. Conversation was not a necessity for them, though, so they were not overly concerned.

They began to cross the dark parking lot, letting the sounds of the party grow more and more distant. The farther they walked, the more slowly they progressed, as they stopped every few feet to share a passionate kiss. Finally, the man resolved to sweep his companion off her feet and carry her to his pickup truck. She giggled with delight and kissed him some more.

"I am so glad I met you tonight," she said.

"Yeah, we seem to be hitting it off alright," the man answered with a grin. Then he paused and looked at her in all seriousness.

"Just so there's no—misunderstanding—you do want to come back to the motel with me, right?"

"Absolutely," said the woman, and she nibbled on the man's earlobe for emphasis. He laughed and pulled out the key to unlock his truck.

The lock popped up and the man reached for the door handle. Then he stopped cold and his breath left him in a frightened shudder.

"What is it?" asked the woman.

The man was suddenly pale and weak and sober. He set the woman back down on her feet with a clumsy and unceremonious motion.

"The plan's off," he said, his voice tight. "Go back inside. Or go home. You can't come with me."

"Well, why on earth?" the woman wailed. "Everything was just fine two minutes ago! Don't I even get an explanation?"

As she voiced her complaints, the man climbed into his truck. He was about to slam the door in the woman's face when he felt a touch of guilt. He had asked the woman to leave with him, so he probably did owe her an explanation. He turned back to her, and in a shaking voice, offered one.

"I just saw 'Skinned Tom,' " he said.

"You saw who?" the woman responded in her too-loud party voice. "Some guy named Tom? 'Cause you look like you saw a ghost."

The man reached out and shook the woman's shoulder with abrupt force.

"Skinned Tom is a ghost!" he hissed. "A warning ghost! Don't tell me you don't know about him!"

"I don't know about him!" the woman insisted. "So let go of me!"

The man released the woman's shoulder. When she began to rub at the sore spot where he had dug his fingers in deeply, he felt another wave of guilt. To ease it, he decided that he would tell the woman the story.

"It happened a long time ago," he said. "Tom was this good-looking guy who lived in the next county over. Same as me. When he was visiting here, he met up with a woman one night. They ended up somewhere—well, somewhere like this, I guess—making out in Tom's car.

"The thing this guy didn't know was that the woman was married. And just as things were really heating up, this great big guy yanks open the car door and drags Tom and his woman friend outside. It was the husband. He didn't do too much to his wife, but he had a knife and he used it on Tom. He made sure that Tom wasn't going to get any more women with his handsome looks. He took that knife and he peeled every square inch of skin off of his face."

The man paused, and looked nervously around before continuing.

"Like I said, Skinned Tom's a ghost now. And when I just went to open up the door of the truck, there…When I looked, and I could see a reflection in the window…" The man stopped and shook his head.

"I saw him," he finally blurted out. "I saw him standing right beside us, with those white eyes staring out of that awful, bloody face. It looked terrible, like raw meat."

"Good Lord," the woman said quietly. She seemed to be several degrees more sober. "You saw that?"

The man nodded. The muscles along his jaw tensed and released rhythmically.

"Well, no wonder you're upset," the woman soothed. Then she moved in closer to the man and placed her hand on his arm. "But I can make you feel better, baby," she said.

The man recoiled instantly.

"Don't you get it?" he hissed. "Skinned Tom doesn't just show himself to everyone! Only as a warning, to guys like me! Guys who are about to get into trouble with a married woman!"

He pushed the woman out of the way then and slammed the door of the truck closed. As he started the engine, she pounded on the window indignantly.

"I'm not married!" she shrieked. "Who told you I was married?"

But the man wasn't listening. He backed out of the parking stall so quickly the woman had to jump back to avoid being struck by the truck's side mirror. Then he sped away, leaving her alone in the most distant corner of the quiet, dark parking lot.

For a minute or two, she watched his tail lights, thinking that he was bound to come to his senses and return for her. When he didn't, she cursed loudly and began walking back toward the honky tonk.

Although it was warm outside, she found herself shivering. She also found herself thinking about the ghost story and feeling more than a little anxious to get back to the comforting lights and company of the bar.

"Skinned Tom," she said with disgust, trying to force herself to dismiss it. But she found that she could not. And she wondered then if Skinned Tom ever acted as more than a ghost of warning. She wondered if he ever acted out of anger, seeking revenge against the woman who had trapped him.

Those were the thoughts passing through the woman's mind as she approached the door of the honky tonk, and they caused her to pause. By the light of the red exit sign, she opened up her purse and took out something that had been carefully wrapped in a tissue. She glanced nervously behind her as she unfolded the tiny package. Inside, there was a ring.

"Leave me alone, Tom," she said in a quivery voice. Then she slipped the ring back onto the third finger of her left hand, opened the door and returned to the party.

The Screaming Bridge

There is a certain small town in the next county where it is tradition for students to have an informal party on graduation night at the little campsite by the bridge. It has been that way for years; for decades, in fact. It always has been and always will be a fine thing to drink bootleg liquor from a paper cup and kiss someone under the stars far from the judging eyes of adults.

Those adults never once tried to put a stop to the campsite party. Maybe it was because they had their own fond post-grad memories. Maybe it was because they saw the get-together as being harmless. Although, the truth is that two terrible things have happened at those parties. One is said to have happened a long time ago. The other happened just this year.

This year, the valedictorian was a fellow named Ted Hobbes. Ted was bright, without being bookish; good-looking, without seeming full of himself; and likeable, despite his obvious wealth of attributes. When he stood by the bonfire that night, all eyes were upon him. Ted handled the spotlight with practiced ease and deflected it frequently and generously upon those who were less popular.

"Why don't you tell us one of your stories, Chris?" he said to a pimply boy who stood half in the shadows.

"Oh, I don't know…" the boy named Chris stammered. He scuffed his feet in the dirt but smiled at the attention.

Ted then told the group that Chris had been in his English class and that he was going to be a great writer one day.

"I don't know about 'great,' " Chris said modestly. Then he brightened with an idea. "Hey, I do know a story that I can tell you, though! A ghost story that takes place right here! Right by this bridge!"

Everyone agreed that a ghost story told beside the campfire would be a perfect idea, and they urged Chris to continue. He took a shy step closer to the flickering flames and told his tale.

"From what I hear, this happened about 30 years ago," he said. "It was graduation night, just like tonight, and all the grads had come here for the party. Most of them were having a good time, but a girl named Brenda Jones was not. Brenda's boyfriend had decided to break up with her and had given her the bad news at the party. Now, I guess she was just nuts over him and she didn't take it too well. They were over there on the riverbank and people up here, at the campsite, could hear her crying and carrying on.

"The boyfriend tried his best to calm Brenda down, but eventually she was so hysterical that she just ran off. This guy was hunting through the bushes on the bank—he got some of his buddies to search too—but they couldn't find her. And then, all of a sudden, they hear this scream from right up there, on the bridge.

"Everybody looked, and there she was. Brenda Jones screamed once, so everyone would look at her, then once more as she did a swan dive into the river.

"From what I heard, they never found her body. This river moves pretty fast and if she did turn up, it would have been a couple hundred miles downstream. Her spirit, though, that stayed right here."

"What do you mean?" asked one of the girls who had been hanging on every word of the story.

"Well—now this is a legend, so I don't know for sure—but they say that when the wind is calm and conditions are just right, you can hear Brenda Jones screaming on her way down to the cold water. Some people even say that she's still trying to get her boyfriend's attention, trying to get him to join her in her watery grave."

The girls all shivered then and cast nervous glances toward the water. The boys laughed and made joking ghostly sounds to prove that the story hadn't affected them one bit. Only Ted Hobbes stood still and quiet, staring thoughtfully into the fire.

"That was creepy," he finally said to Chris. "Good story, man."

But Ted didn't really look as though he had enjoyed the tale and, in an antisocial move that was unlike him, he turned away from his friends and went down to the river where he could be alone.

Five minutes later, he was back. There was dirt on his white pullover, from having clawed his way quickly up the bank, and an expression of terror on his face.

"Did you hear that?" he asked in a panicked voice. "Did any of you hear that, just a minute ago?"

All the young people who weren't too busy necking shrugged and looked at each other and said that they hadn't heard anything unusual.

Ted stared at them in disbelief.

"You had to have heard it!" he said. "It was a scream! Someone was screaming over on the bridge!"

They all laughed then and congratulated Ted on having made such a good effort to frighten them. But nobody was about to fall for an improvisational version of the story of Brenda Jones's doomed ghost.

Ted denied fabricating the story, but as he looked from one bemused face to the next, he began to doubt himself.

"Maybe my imagination did get the better of me," he admitted. But no more than a few seconds later, he jumped as though he had been touched with a live wire.

"There it is again!" he yelled. "That scream!"

Again, Ted Hobbes found himself alone. If anyone else had heard the cry of distress, they weren't admitting to it.

"Someone's in trouble," Ted said. "We have to help." When no one offered to accompany him, he shook his head in disappointment and set off alone.

For the next two hours, the partygoers watched uneasily as Ted scoured every inch of the bridge and surrounding riverbank, searching for the source of the screams that only he could hear. He looked around the pylons, behind every steel girder, and combed the entire bridge deck. At times, he appeared ready to give up, but then his head would snap back and he would call out "I hear you! I'm coming! Tell me where you are!" Frequently, Ted's best friends pleaded with him to rejoin them at the campsite. Occasionally, someone would try to approach him and take his arm. He reacted so wildly to such attempts that everyone thought it best to keep their distance, lest their obsessed friend lose his footing and fall.

Many people left the party early. Near dawn, those who remained were forced to admit that Ted had come unglued and that some authoritative adult intervention was required. They decided to call upon a friendly, middle-aged police officer whom they affectionately referred to as "Copper."

"Copper can get Ted down off the bridge," one of the kids nodded confidently. "And he'll probably be willing to keep it quiet." No one wanted to see Ted's fine reputation and prospects blemished because of a few too many graduation-night beers.

Someone went off to rouse Copper out of bed. The others sat on the riverbank and watched Ted's frantic search. At one point, he lay down flat on his belly, hanging dangerously over the edge of the bridge deck, so that he could peer at the network of steel support beams that were beneath it. The pose looked so precarious that a few of the boys who were watching jumped to their feet.

"Ted!" one shouted. "Get back!"

"No, I can see her!" was his reply. Then, to whoever was supposedly trapped in the beams beneath the bridge, he called out, "I see you now! Give me your hand! Just a little closer…Give me your…"

And then Ted Hobbes leaned too far forward and lost his grip. He screamed horribly as he plunged into the black waters below.

Copper arrived five minutes later, which, of course, was much too late. There was nothing that he, or anyone else, could do. As had been pointed out earlier, it was a fast-moving river and Ted's body would already have been far downstream.

Chris, the acne-plagued youth who had told the story, was perhaps the most distraught. He confided to Copper that he would never have imagined a fellow like Ted having such an irrational reaction to something like the old folktale about Brenda Jones.

The policeman nodded in solemn agreement, but corrected the boy on one point.

"You know, the story's actually true," he said. "Well, the ghost part is probably a lot of hogwash," he admitted with a shrug, "but the girl diving off the bridge—now, that really happened. It was a long time ago. Before I was even on the force."

Chris then asked the obvious question.

"If Brenda Jones was real," he said, "who was the guy who jilted her?"

Copper stopped still for a moment then. When he turned to face the boy beside him, his eyebrows were raised in an expression of vague surprise.

"Well, now, that's an odd coincidence," he said. And then Copper told Chris and the others the name of the fellow over whom Brenda Jones had killed herself. It was a name they all recognized, but not because of the man's business connections, or his good standing with the Rotary Club, or his seat on the town's council. They knew him, first and foremost, because he was the father of a friend.

His name was Dan Hobbes. And his son—drawn into a watery grave prepared by his own father's actions at a graduation party years earlier—was Ted.

The Scratching

One summer evening, a teenaged couple who had told their parents that they were going to a movie drove up to a place called Lookout Point. There were several other cars parked at the roadside turnout with the unforgettable view. The boy drove deliberately past them all and turned down a hidden, overgrown little trail to a dark, remote place where the girl had never been.

"Why can't we just park back there, with everyone else?" she asked nervously as they drove along and branches whipped against the windows of the car.

"There's bound to be someone who knows us back there," the boy explained. "Do you want your parents to find out we didn't go to the movie?"

The girl had to admit that she did not. So she put away her objections, freshened her lipstick, and told herself that even if something frightening was to happen, her boyfriend was there to keep her safe.

Half an hour later, however, he was determined to leave the car.

"Where are you going?" the girl cried when the boy reached for the door handle.

"I have to go to the bathroom," he complained as he pulled free of her clinging hands. "Let me go; I'll be just a minute."

With a mocking grin, the boy stepped out of the car. He slammed the door behind him and vanished into the deep shadows within seconds.

He'll be just a minute, the girl told herself. *He'll be right back.* But her boyfriend did not return immediately and it became more difficult for her to keep her fears at bay. She was unaccustomed to the night noises of the forest and imagined that each one represented a threat. Every rustling of the bushes was a wild animal, ready to pounce; every sigh of the breeze was the wheezing breath of the escaped, knife-wielding murderer who was said to stake out such desolate places in search of easy prey. Finally, she could not stand to be alone in the company of her imagination any longer.

"I'll give you one more minute!" she called out the window to her boyfriend. "One more minute, and then I'm leaving!" She started the car's engine for emphasis, and slid over to the driver's seat. There, she watched the seconds tick by on the dashboard's digital clock.

The minute passed and the girl grew indignant. *He knows that I'm nervous out here,* she thought. *How dare he deliberately frighten me!* As she rolled the window up, she screamed out into the darkness that what she was about to do was her boyfriend's own fault. Then she put the car into gear.

But the ground was soft and the tires spun hopelessly, managing to do nothing more than send up a spray of mud. The girl tried to drive forward and then in reverse. The car wouldn't budge either way. Finally, she gave up. She turned the motor off and collapsed tearfully against the seat.

"Alright, I'm sorry!" she sobbed through the small window opening. "Now, please come back! You've scared me enough!" But there came no answer from the shadowy, tangled brush.

There was no answer—but there was a sound. A scratching sound. The first scratch caught the young girl's attention. The second time she heard it, she was able to pinpoint its origin. It was coming from the roof of the car. Something, or someone, was on the roof.

Cold terror jolted through the girl's body. In a flurry of frantic motion, she checked all of the door locks and rolled up the window that she had left just slightly open. She froze then and tried to stifle the sound of her own jagged breath so that she could listen.

Scratch. It was definitely coming from the roof of the car.

The girl reasoned that the sound might be nothing more than a low branch of one of the many towering trees that surrounded the car, or perhaps a rodent or other small animal. None of this reasoning made her feel better, though. None of it could stop her from hyperventilating or slow her racing pulse. The problem was that, even if she could explain away the creepy scratching, she could not find a logical way to explain the continued absence of her boyfriend, who had now been gone for more than half an hour.

Unless, she thought…*unless he's having some fun with me.*

The very thought infuriated her. Anger felt better than fear, so the girl nurtured it. Every time she heard the scratching noise, she imagined her boyfriend hiding behind a tree, using a long branch to scrape the roof of the car and frighten her out of her wits.

As the girl's outrage grew, so did her resolve to not let the boy get the better of her. She was still too anxious to leave the car, and not eager to make the long walk back to the public road, but there was no reason that she should not have a decent night's sleep. The girl crawled into the back seat, where she wrapped herself in an old blanket and eventually fell into an uneasy state of unconsciousness.

The dreams that she had were terrible. Monsters with wild eyes stared at her through the car windows, and their faces were twisted into expressions of sneering laughter. The long, broken claws of some unseen creature scraped time and time again across the roof of the car, leaving a trail of dull, gray scars in the metallic paint. The girl even dreamed that she was again trying to drive the car back to the road. In her dream, as in reality, she was unsuccessful; but in her dream it was because her boyfriend had punctured all four of the tires with a long, jagged knife.

When she finally woke, the girl was tremendously relieved to see the pale light of dawn. Knowing that there was nothing to be afraid of by the light of day, she opened the car door and swung her legs out into the fresh morning air. She was just about to stand up when she saw something familiar only a short distance away from her feet.

It was a navy-blue sneaker, one of her boyfriend's shoes. It lay on the ground, resting by the gnarly root of a tree. The girl could see that its white shoe lace was still neatly tied.

The girl stood up. But before she could reach for the mysteriously abandoned shoe, or do anything else, she was startled by the sound of a vehicle that came crashing through the underbrush toward her.

It was a police cruiser. The two officers obviously had not expected to encounter another vehicle in their path, for they wore expressions of shock. They brought the cruiser to a stop only a few yards behind the car in which the young girl had just spent the night, and the one who had been driving leapt out.

"Come here!" he shouted. "Walk to me, quickly. And whatever you do, don't look back!"

"I know we shouldn't have parked here," explained the girl, "but the car is stuck and…"

"You're not in trouble!" the officer assured her. "Just, please, come here and don't look back!"

As the girl grew closer to the cruiser, she was better able to read the emotion that was written on the faces of the policemen. It wasn't annoyance at having had to spend a night searching for a couple of stupid teenaged kids. It was horror. Suddenly, the girl's knees were weak, and her stomach had formed a cold knot below her ribs.

She found herself thinking about the lone shoe, and despite what the police officer had warned her, she turned around.

It was then that the girl saw where her boyfriend had spent the night. He was bound, gagged and hanging upside-down from the branches of a tall tree. His body had been suspended directly above the roof of the car.

He was dead; that was obvious. It was also obvious that he had not died immediately. The girl could see that her boyfriend had survived long enough to free one of his hands from the loops of thick rope. He had used that hand to try to signal for her help.

Just then, a slight gust of wind caused the corpse to sway ever so slightly. The dead boy's fingernails, which were worn, and broken, and embedded with metallic automotive paint, dragged slowly across the roof of the car.

The familiar scratching sound was the last thing the girl heard before she fainted.

The Weeping Woman

Long ago, there was a woman who was abandoned by her husband and left to raise three small children on her own. The family was poor and times were hard; often they were hungry and cold. The woman was lonely and longed for companionship. When a certain man showed interest in courting her, she did all she could to attract him.

Unfortunately, he was only interested in the woman. Since the three children were not his own, he did not particularly want them about, and he definitely balked at the expense of feeding so many mouths. The woman knew this and assumed it to be the problem when her suitor's attention began to wither.

If I am left alone with the children again, we will all four starve, she reasoned. *But I have been given a chance to save myself.* With this horrible, ill-conceived logic, she gathered her children and set out for the river.

It was a cold, rainy night and an icy wind howled around the huddled foursome. The children begged their mother to be allowed to return to the fireside, where it was warm and dry. She refused, saying that there was a bit of important business to attend to first.

The business was murder. The woman took her small children to the highest cliff that rose above the river and threw them, one by one, into the churning, cold water. When she was finished, she wept, but quickly consoled herself with the knowledge that she would at least keep her man, and that she could always have more children.

She soon discovered, however, that her lover's decreasing interest had less to do with the children than it did with her. As the weeks passed, he stayed away more often and complained more frequently about little things that the woman did. Then, one day, he simply did not come to see her. The woman had been abandoned by yet another man.

It was then that the woman truly felt regret for her actions. Day and night, she wept for her dead children. Often, she walked by the riverside while she mourned, torturing herself with thoughts of how their poor little bodies had been swept away by the current. One dark evening, in the midst of a violent thunderstorm, she came to a conclusion.

"I must find my babies, or I will never have peace!" she cried. Then, struggling against the wind and rain, the woman climbed to the high cliff where she had killed her children. With one final, forlorn cry, she threw herself headlong into the raging river.

It should have been the end of her. But it was not.

Many people who lived near the river began to tell tales of a sorrowful figure, clad in a flowing, black dress, who skimmed smoothly over the rocky ground near their homes on stormy nights. It was a terrible thing to hear her lament, they said. But there were others who claimed that there was something even more terrible about her.

"She steals children," they said solemnly. And they told horrifying stories of little ones who had been playing by the water's edge when the grieving black spirit approached them. Once coaxed into her spectral arms, those youngsters had been forever lost to their own loving parents. If their lifeless bodies ever were found, it was in the weed-choked water near the riverbank, where the wraith had discarded them.

It has been more than a hundred years now. Still, this phantom has found no peace, for she has yet to find her murdered children. She may be doomed to search forever, which is why everyone must beware. For when her own children are not in sight, it seems that any child will do. The woman once comforted herself with the thought that she could always have more children, and now it seems she means to have yours.

So, don't let your little sons and daughters wander near the water, and warn them of the dangers that lurk in the wildest, stormy nights. Keep your children indoors, close and safe, and teach them to never approach a certain pitiful figure who cries woefully into the wind. If you fail to do this, they may some-day vanish within the black embrace of the eternally weeping woman.

A Grave Mistake

There is a nearby town where a secret sorority of young women exists. To become a member is a great honor and provides a girl with many benefits and advantages. But, of course, becoming a member is not easy. First, the candidate must be nominated by one of the senior members. Second, and more difficult, the proposed member must pass an initiation proving that she is courageous beyond doubt.

That initiation is always the same. The girl who wishes to join is told to present herself to the sorority leaders on the night of a full moon. She is given a hooded cloak to wear, a sturdy leather belt to cinch it, and a sheathed dagger that hangs from the belt. The girl is then driven to a field several miles from the town. She is directed to a dense copse of trees in the corner of that field. Everyone for miles around knows that field and those trees. They surround a small family burial ground that is known to be haunted. To pass the initiation, the girl must spend one hour in the cemetery, and then, before she leaves, plunge the dagger deeply into the soil of the oldest grave there.

Many girls, upon learning the details of their proposed initiation, have walked away from the sorority and never looked back. Others nervously agreed to spend their hour among the tombstones and often ended up with terrifying tales to tell. But once, there

was a girl named Rebecca who accepted the challenge with confidence so great that it bordered on arrogance. Later, everyone wished that she had been one of those who walked away.

Rebecca wanted very much to belong to the prestigious sorority and, perhaps, she wanted to impress the members with her bravado.

"Is that all I have to do?" she asked when the initiation was explained to her. "That's nothing! If I was superstitious, I might be worried, but anyone sensible knows that there's no such thing as a ghost!"

The older girls, who had each spent their frightening hour in the graveyard, disagreed. They had seen and heard things there that could not be explained. They all remained silent, however, knowing that on the night of the next full moon, Rebecca would form a different opinion.

When that night came, the sky was clear and the moon glowed like a polished silver dollar. The shadows of the trees stretched out like long dark fingers. As the sorority approached the cemetery, many of the girls were visibly anxious. Rebecca maintained her cool facade.

"You must spend one full hour within the cemetery fence," instructed the leader. "No matter what happens, it is imperative that you stay."

"During that time," said another girl, "you should read the dates on each of the tombstones."

"Find the oldest grave there," spoke a third, "and then, when the alarm clock rings to signal the end of the hour, you must plunge the dagger into that grave!"

"Then you may leave," all of the girls spoke together, "if the angered spirits will let you."

They set the clock then and watched as Rebecca climbed over the fence and walked away.

Rebecca watched them until their dark shapes blended in with the trees at the edge of the field.

"Piece of cake," she muttered to herself as she turned to face the graves.

She had to admit that the little burial ground looked haunted. The aged tombstones leaned this way and that, and there were a few crude wooden markers that had been nearly worn away by the elements. Tall trees loomed over the graves like stern sentinels, and the fence that surrounded the entire scene was rotting and decrepit. Still, Rebecca reminded herself, looking haunted and being haunted were two entirely different things. She couldn't allow herself to give in to hysterical imaginings.

But the moonlight tended to play tricks on one's eyes. Rebecca jumped on several occasions when a shadow in the periphery of her vision moved stealthily. Once, a white shape, which was surely a cloud of vapor escaping from the marshy ground, floated over the graves and amongst the trees. And the normally benign sounds of the night—hooting owls, swooping bats and scurrying rodents—were somehow frightening when a person couldn't pinpoint their exact origin. Through it all, though, Rebecca kept a calm head and read the time-ravaged inscriptions on the grave markers.

By the end of the hour, she had found what she was looking for.

"Silas Cooke," she said aloud. "It looks like you've been here the longest. Try not to be offended, but in a couple of minutes I will have to treat you in a most disrespectful manner."

Perhaps it was a slight breeze, but Rebecca felt as though an icy hand touched her spine then. A mouse ran over her foot, making her flesh crawl, and some insect buzzed insolently into the loose hood of her dark robe. Frantically, she swept the hood off her head and swatted at her hair until her ears rang. No more than 10 seconds after the bug left, the alarm rang out, fracturing the silence and causing Rebecca to jump once more.

"Let's get this over with," she whispered as she unsheathed the dagger and knelt down on Silas Cooke's grave. Then she called out the name of the sorority, raised her arms high above her head, and plunged the dagger deep into the cold earth.

All of the fear that Rebecca had been unwilling to acknowledge rose up to greet her at that moment. The very instant that the blade was imbedded, she felt electric panic take hold of her senses. Suddenly, she needed to run, escape, leap over the fractured fence and flee the horrible little cemetery with its overgrown graves and moss-covered stones. But when she tried to do that, when she tried to jump up from the grave that she had just desecrated, something clutched at her, pulling her back down.

In Rebecca's terrified mind, it could only have been the furious wraith of Silas Cooke. Motivated by pure horror, she tried, once more, to flee. But before she even made it to her feet, she was seized from behind and yanked back down. Rebecca, the sensible girl who had assumed that spirits did not exist, suddenly knew without a doubt that a cold, skeletal hand had reached up through the soil to exact revenge for her act of defilement.

The other girls were walking back across the field when they heard the scream. It was ear-splitting and dreadful, enough to shock them into forgetting about their solemn ritual. They let loose screams of their own and ran back to the road and the safety of their vehicle. It was more than an hour before they mustered the courage to once again approach the cemetery and search for their new friend.

When they found Rebecca, she was as dead as the corpses that had kept her company in the last hour of her life. Her eyes were wide and staring, and her face was twisted into an expression of absolute horror. Her lips remained parted in their final scream. She was sprawled over the grave of Silas Cooke.

That she had died of fright was obvious. Exactly why was a mystery. At least it was until the girls tried to move Rebecca's lifeless body from the grave.

"Wait," said one of them. "Something's caught."

And, indeed, something was. The flowing black fabric of the robe Rebecca had been wearing was firmly pinned to the ground…pinned by the dagger that the girl had used to violate Silas Cooke's grave…

The Helpful Stranger

A woman had just spent the evening shopping at a local mall. When the stores closed, she gathered her bags of purchases and walked across the deserted parking garage. It was a dark night, and the empty parkade was a shadowy, frightening place. As she listened to the echo of her own footfalls, she resolved that in the future she would either leave the mall earlier or park closer to the entrance.

The woman's feelings of unease grew more extreme once she reached her car, for she found it waiting for her with a flat tire. She debated returning to the mall to call for help, but decided against it.

I can probably change the tire in less time than it would take me to backtrack, she reasoned. So she opened the trunk, took out the jack and the spare tire and set to work.

Fifteen minutes later, she was regretting her decision. Her hands were numb with cold and not strong enough to loosen the lug nuts on the damaged tire. The woman was just about to give up when she heard a man's voice behind her.

"May I help you with that?"

The woman gasped in shock and spun around. She had not heard a single sound to warn her that anyone had been approaching. When she looked, she was relieved to see a clean-cut man in a business suit, carrying a sleek and expensive-looking briefcase.

"You know, I could use a hand," the woman admitted, and she gratefully handed over her wrench. "Thank you for offering."

The man smiled and set his briefcase in the trunk of the car.

"It's no problem," he assured her. "Won't take a minute."

And truly, it did not. The man changed the tire with ease and put the tools and the flat away in the trunk. He closed the trunk firmly then and turned around. He grinned and dusted his hands off in an exaggerated fashion.

"All finished," he said grandly.

The woman thanked him again and offered to pay, but the man gallantly refused any compensation.

"But there is something else you could do for me," he admitted as he looked at his watch. "I'm running late now, and my car is parked on the other side of the mall. Would you mind driving me over there?"

The woman felt uncomfortable letting a total stranger into her vehicle but didn't want to seem ungrateful. So, instead of answering the man directly, she stalled by asking him a teasing question.

"Now, if your car's over there, what were you doing wandering around out here?" she laughed. "Were you actively searching for damsels in distress?"

The stranger didn't laugh. In fact, the woman noted that for a second his eyes turned cold and hard. It was only a second, though, and then he smiled and offered a reasonable explanation.

"I was with a friend," he said. "Her car was parked in this lot. I didn't want her to walk out here unescorted."

It seemed so plausible and so gallant that the woman felt ashamed of her suspicious nature. She lowered her eyes in embarrassment, nodded and moved to unlock her car's passenger-side door. But as she was about to insert the key in the lock, she saw the man's shoes. They weren't the sort of shoes that anyone wore with a tailored business suit. They were soft and rubber-soled, shoes that someone would wear if he worked the night shift in a hospital. Shoes that someone would wear if he wanted to sneak up on people in deserted parking garages.

Suddenly, the woman's heart was beating very quickly.

"You know, I'd like to help you," she said as she withdrew her keys and dropped them back in her purse, "but I just remembered something. Something that I forgot, back in the mall."

She turned then and ran back toward the lights of the distant shopping center. The only sounds she heard were her own pounding pulse and the echo of her shoes striking the concrete floor. There were no sounds of pursuing footsteps, but that was no comfort. The stealthy stranger in his quiet, rubber-soled shoes could have been only a few feet away.

The woman made it through the entrance doors and found the mall's security station. She told her story to one of the uniformed guards and felt quite foolish by the time she reached the end of it.

"I've probably let my imagination run wild," she said sheepishly. "A person really shouldn't be persecuted for doing good deeds in comfortable shoes. But still, if you wouldn't mind walking me to my car, I'd feel much more safe."

The guard said that he didn't mind. He escorted the woman back to her vehicle. By that time, the man who had changed the flat tire was nowhere to be seen.

The woman shook her head as she looked around.

"I really feel terrible now," she said. "That poor man's probably late, all because of me, and…oh, no!"

She had glanced at the rear of the car while she spoke, and was hit with a flash of memory.

"His briefcase!" she said to the security guard. "He left it in the trunk! This is awful!"

The woman fished her keys out of her purse and opened the trunk. As she had guessed, the stranger's slim attache case was sitting next to the tools and the flat tire.

The security guard shone his flashlight over the contents of the trunk.

"Don't worry," he told the woman. "We can get this back to him. There's probably some identification in here."

He pressed a button near the latch and the case sprang open. Both the security guard and the woman stood in shocked silence then, as they viewed what was inside. It was not the identification that they had been looking for, but it told them far more than any piece of identification could.

The briefcase held nothing but a long coil of nylon rope and a knife.

"Oh, my God!" the woman whispered. "Does he just wander around with this stuff, waiting for someone's car to break down?"

"I don't think so," said the guard, and he pointed to a tiny, third item in the briefcase.

It was the missing valve stem from the woman's flat tire.

The Telephantom

There is a certain unsettling story that has been told for many years. Sometimes it is said to be about a retired British businessman. Sometimes the teller claims that the subject was a wealthy American entrepreneur. All agree upon the details, however— the frightening thing that happened.

The story took place in the 1930s, and the gentleman in question was said to be comfortably wealthy. All of his money, however, did nothing to quell his greatest fear: the fear that he would someday be buried alive.

As the man advanced in years, he did the one thing that he could do to ensure that he would not be prematurely entombed with no means of escape. He stipulated that a functioning telephone be installed in the crypt in which he was to be interred. It relieved his anxiety somewhat to know that if the worst was to happen, he could simply call for help.

Eventually, the day came when the man passed away. A funeral was held and the casket was walled up next to the telephone inside the expensive marble mausoleum. Naturally, the man's relatives never received any emergency calls from the crypt, and the eccentric telephone installation was forgotten.

When two years had passed, there came a day when a member of the family became concerned about the dead man's widow. She lived alone, and for several hours there had been a constant busy signal on her telephone. The relative finally went to the house to see if anything was the matter. He arrived to find his worst fears confirmed.

The woman was dead. It was assumed that her heart had stopped, owing to some terrible fright, for her features had been frozen in an expression of absolute horror. Clutched tightly in her hand was the telephone receiver, which had been off the hook for several hours.

There was another funeral then, and another casket that had to be placed within the family crypt. When the door was unsealed to admit the woman's remains, what the family saw gave them a great shock.

The receiver of the telephone, which sat inside the sealed mausoleum, was resting on the top of the table. Though no one had been inside the marble tomb for two years, the phone had been taken off the hook.

Part Two
Stories Told by Moonlight

*Since the beginning of time, certain feelings have been
evoked by the pale, eerie light of the full moon. That
silvery, shimmering disk has inspired stories of spirits
and monsters and all manner of supernatural creatures.*

*When the mood calls for a frightening tale, and you wish to
revisit traditional themes, bask in the glow of the lunar
lady. It is time for a story told by moonlight…*

Wolf Water

One summer, a wealthy farmer invited his cousin from the city to come and live with his family. The cousin was an unmarried young woman with an adventurous spirit and a disrespectful tongue, and to tell the truth, the farmer did not care for her. But his aunt, for whom he had great affection, had begged him to take her in.

"A summer in the country will make her more sensible," said the aunt, "and I would consider your invitation a great favor."

And so the cousin came to stay.

Almost immediately, the farmer regretted his decision. The girl brought suitcases filled with ridiculous, inappropriate clothing, and suddenly his own daughters were no longer satisfied with their own modest wardrobes. She flirted endlessly with his sons, and the farmer had to be twice as stern with them to help them keep their minds on their chores. Worst of all, the cousin was so fond of attention that she told wildly fantastic stories, which the farmer's children accepted as true.

"I was out walking today," began one of her tales, told at the dinner table on a night shortly after her arrival, "and I came upon the clearest, coolest little stream. You must know it—it cuts through the distant corner of your land, near the woods."

The farmer's children looked at one another and shrugged their shoulders. They were generally discouraged from wandering and had not been to the outskirts of their father's property because their chores did not take them there.

"Well," continued the cousin, "I had a long drink of that water and noticed that it had a most peculiar, metallic taste. When I arrived back home, I mentioned this to your farmhand and he turned as pale as milk. He told me that I had just drunk from the wolves' watering hole. 'And you know what happens to them what drinks wolf water, miss,' he said to me. 'They turns into werewolves!' "

The cousin laughed with delight then, as though the prospect of transforming into a werewolf was immensely entertaining. The farmer scowled to show his disapproval.

"That man is a strong worker, but a superstitious idiot," he snapped. "My children don't listen to his stories and neither should you. And I don't want such rubbish spoken of in this house again!"

The cousin winked and clucked her tongue, and looked at the farmer in a teasing manner.

"Perhaps you're afraid of me now, dear cousin?" she said. "Now that I have the potential to become a wild beast?"

"Wolves are no laughing matter," the farmer said. "Not to anyone who has invested heavily in livestock!"

He slammed his hand on the table to show that the matter was closed.

The cousin didn't mind. There were countless subjects with which she was able to torment the farmer. She didn't need to stick with any particular one.

❦ ❦ ❦

The weeks went by and the farmer's misery intensified. One day, his cousin taught his youngest daughter to apply makeup like a showgirl. On another day, she was discovered kissing the son of the local preacher, who had come to the farm seeking contributions for the church. She showed no respect for the farmer's authority or his rules, and caused him embarrassment on a daily basis. To relieve his stress, the farmer complained about her to anyone who would listen.

"She's a terrible girl," he told his neighbor. "She's causing great disruption in my house."

"I should never have invited her," he said to the shopkeeper. "She'll ruin my reputation yet."

"I've never heard such wild lies in all my life," he confided to the sheriff. "You can't believe a word that comes out of that girl's mouth."

Eventually, however, the farmer had to turn his attention to a new problem. The wolves in the county had become much more bold and fierce, and they were regularly stealing lambs from his flock. One day, as the farmer spoke of the problem to his wife, his cousin overheard.

"Problems with wolves?" she goaded him. "Perhaps they are still angry that I drank their water."

"It's no joke!" the farmer shouted, and he stormed out of the room. Then silently he resolved that he would take action to solve his problem before the month's end.

*　*　*

On the first night of the full moon, the farmer loaded his rifle and hid himself away in the loft of the barn. From his vantage point, with the bright clear light of the moon, he had a fine view of all the animals in their pens and he would be able to see any predators well in advance of their arrival on the scene.

"Now, let the beast show itself," he muttered as he settled down to watch. But hours passed and nothing happened. Eventually, the farmer drifted off to sleep.

He awoke to the tortured cry of a fat lamb.

"What? Who's there?" the farmer sputtered as he jolted into consciousness. Then he opened his eyes and looked out over the animals. What he saw nearly shocked him into dropping his rifle.

It was a wolf, but not a wolf of the ordinary sort that he had been expecting. It was the largest beast that the farmer had ever seen. The creature stood as many hands high as a pony he had once given his children. It had a head that was massive and thick. But none of this disturbed the farmer as much as the sight of the monster clutching a large wounded lamb in its two front paws, while balancing perfectly well on its hindquarters.

"Good Lord," whispered the farmer as he raised his rifle and peered through the sight.

The wolf appeared to hear him. It turned its attention from the prey in its claws and looked up to the loft of the barn with eyes that had the dull red glow of two small hot coals. Then its jaws parted in what looked for all the world to the farmer like a smile, a most familiar, mocking smile.

The farmer took careful aim and squeezed the trigger.

The animal dropped the lamb and bellowed out in pain. A dark, liquid stain began to run down its matted fur, spreading to the left and right as the wolf writhed. As the stain grew larger, the wolf somehow seemed to grow smaller. When the beast finally fell to the ground, it no longer dwarfed the slain lamb that lay beside it.

How can it be? the farmer thought. He felt that he could no longer believe what he saw with his own two eyes. Next he doubted his ears, as the wolf let out a final anguished cry that sounded more like a human lament. Then, with a smaller sound, strangely reminiscent of soft laughter, the creature perished.

The farmer was shaking when he descended from the loft and walked over to examine his kill. He had used his rifle on barnyard predators before, but never on anything so fearsome. He needed to see the animal up close, to assure himself that it was truly dead and no longer a threat.

Perhaps I'll mount the head, he thought, *and display it in my study.* But as he drew closer to the crumpled body lying in the corner of the barnyard, he knew that would never come to pass.

There was no wolf there. Only the naked mud- and blood-streaked corpse of his cousin.

The farmer dropped his rifle to the ground.

"What has happened? How could such a thing happen?" he muttered as he surveyed the tragic scene. And then it occurred to him that what would happen *next* was far more of a concern.

By the time people were eating their noon meal on the following day, the story had spread throughout the county.

"It's a shame," the preacher declared solemnly. "Judgment was not his to pass."

"They had plenty of differences, but that was no way to settle them," said the neighbor as he shook his head.

"This will ruin the whole family's reputation," sighed the shopkeeper.

When the sheriff came to lay the charge of murder, the farmer was wild-eyed and full of insane explanations.

"Don't you see?" he pleaded. "It must have been true! It must have been true, what she said about the wolf water!"

The sheriff shook his head soberly, tightened the handcuffs on the farmer's wrists and led him out of the house. Once he had placed the accused man securely in the back of his car, he turned to his deputy and sighed.

"It must be a family failing," he said. "The wild tales and all. You can't believe a word that comes out of that man's mouth."

And with that, they took the farmer away.

An Ungodly Mess

The boy was 13 and the girl was 11. That was entirely too old to be cared for by a babysitter, they had told their mother at the beginning of summer vacation.

"Save your money," they had said, because they knew that saving money justified almost anything to a single parent who worked long hours for little pay. In the end they managed to convince her because they agreed to follow a list of rules and promised to clean up after themselves.

The rules, they were pretty good about. The housekeeping was a different matter.

"Every day when I come home, I am faced with this ungodly mess!" the mother complained. Her complaints affected the children little. But when she threatened to revoke their newfound independence by hiring a sitter after all, they paid attention.

"We're sorry," said the boy.

"We'll do better," said the girl.

And they did try. But on occasion, despite their best intentions, a mess would just happen.

One day, they made triple-decker peanut butter and jelly sandwiches for an afternoon snack. When they were finished, they looked around the kitchen and saw that there were bread crumbs littering the floor and smears of grape jelly on the counter.

"This is no good," said the girl.

"I suppose we have to clean it up," agreed the boy. He handed his sister the dustpan and broom, and took the dishcloth off its hook, so that he could wipe up the counter.

When he turned on the faucet to dampen the cloth, however, he let out a cry of disgust.

"Eww! Gross!" he said, and quickly leapt back from the sink.

His sister asked what the matter was, and the boy showed her his hand.

"Eww! Gross!" she concurred.

Clinging to the boy's fingers was a purplish black, thick, gelatinous substance.

"It came out of the tap," he explained as he wiped the goo away with the dishcloth. The blob came off easily, but left a deep stain on the boy's skin.

The girl turned the faucet on, so she could see it for herself. There was a rattling sound from deep within the pipes, and then a hiss of trapped air. Then, just as the boy had claimed, a thick, shiny rope of the mystery substance came oozing out of the tap.

The children stared at the glistening mucus in disbelief. They had seen the water get a little brown sometimes during the spring runoff, but never that dark. And never thick.

The girl reached over to shut the tap off, but her brother stopped her.

"Maybe we should let it run awhile," he suggested. "You know, to let the gunk clear out."

It seemed to be a sensible solution, so the girl agreed. For several minutes, the brother and sister stood in the middle of the kitchen floor and watched the strange slime flow into the big stainless-steel sink. They waited to hear a final sputtering cough from the pipes, signaling that the water was about to run fresh and clear. But there was no sound, there came no clean water, and after a while, it became obvious that the goo was running into the sink faster than it was draining out. The basin had begun to fill up with the stuff. Finally, with a sigh, the boy reached over and shut the faucet off.

"Is it clogged, do you think?" the girl asked.

"Probably. Great. That's one more mess to clean up," said the boy.

"Maybe it just needs a little stirring," the girl suggested. She took a wooden spoon out of the dish rack and poked very gingerly at the shimmery, trembling mass in the sink. A membrane had formed upon the surface of it and it dimpled down beneath the touch of the spoon. When the girl pushed a little harder and the spoon broke through, it burst like a ripe berry. Deep purple juice splattered upward, dotting the girl's hand and wrist.

"There we go," she said as she began to stir. There was a sucking sound from deep within the drain. After several minutes of stirring and coaxing, though, the level of slime seemed to be no lower.

The boy had been about to mention that fact when something else caught his attention.

"Look at this," he said to his sister as he held up his hand.

What she saw caused her to furrow her brow.

"I thought you wiped it off," she said.

The boy nodded. He had wiped it off. But strangely, on the stained places on his hand, there clung several large globules of the substance. They quivered as the boy moved his fingers.

"I think they're growing," he said. His features twisted into an expression of revulsion and he frantically flicked his wrist several times. With a soft slapping sound, the small blobs struck the kitchen wall. Slowly, they began to slide downwards, leaving juicy purple slug trails behind them. Neither the boy nor the girl noticed, however. They were too busy gaping at what was happening to the boy's hand.

Where the boy had just shaken the shiny drops off his hand, more had begun to blossom. The thick substance oozed out of his pores in rivulets and ran together like quicksilver. He wiped at the spots again and again. Each time the slime was replaced a little more rapidly.

"It's coming out of me!" he shrieked. "How can it be coming out of me?"

The more quickly the goo reproduced, the more obvious the answer became. Brother and sister both squealed in horror as they watched the blob expand and the flesh beneath it shrink.

"It's eating me! It's eating me!" he cried. His hand had begun to look extraordinarily thin; skeletal, in fact. Loose skin draped over stick-like fingers with bulging knuckles. The purplish black stuff, in comparison, was expanding at such a rate that great masses of it began dropping to the linoleum with wet plopping noises. When it hit, it splattered its dark juice on the boy's white sweat socks. Ominous stains spread across the cotton and he could feel the dampness attacking his feet.

"I'm calling Mom!" the girl sobbed. One of the strict rules of the house was that the children were never to phone their mother at work, except in the case of an emergency. The girl grabbed the telephone without hesitation, certain that they had reached that state.

But her fingers felt odd when she tried to punch the numbers. They seemed weak and sticky. The girl pulled her hand away from the phone and was sickened to see that the pads of her fingers remained glued to the handset. In place of fingertips, she had developed open sores that dripped something too thick and dark and oily to be blood.

"I can't…" she tried to say, but suddenly speech had become difficult. Her tongue had, without warning, become soft and useless.

"I know…" responded her brother, but the words came out as wet, guttural noises with no meaning. When his lips parted, a ribbon of blackish drool ran out of the corner of his mouth, slid down his neck, and snaked inside the collar of his shirt.

The boy's body was shrinking, caving inward. He felt his ribs turn into something spongy as he collapsed into a soft heap in front of the refrigerator. He looked helplessly up at his sister, who was clinging to a kitchen stool and making wet smacking noises with every struggling motion. Her eyes met his, and for a moment he thought she was crying. Then he realized that it was a trickle of slime seeping out of her tear duct.

Within 10 minutes of turning on the faucet, even their clothing was gone. In its place was a large, slithering mound of dark gelatin. With great sucking sounds, it dragged itself laboriously across the kitchen floor and squished behind the appliances, where it would wait until another came to join it.

* * *

The mother arrived home at six o'clock as usual. She took one look around the kitchen and shook her head in disappointment. The peanut butter and jelly jars sat open on the countertop, and the bread had been unwrapped and left to turn stale. Crumbs littered the small Formica table. Worst of all, though, dark purple smears of grape jelly covered the counter, the sink and even the floor.

The mother took off her coat, sighed and rummaged in the cabinet beneath the sink for a sponge.

"What an ungodly mess," she muttered as she turned on the faucet.

Sandman

For as long as anyone who lived in the little village by the lake could remember, there had been stories of the Sandman. Not the friendly, fairytale creature who sprinkled dream dust into a person's eyes; no, not that one at all. The village's Sandman was a dark thing, a thing to be feared. He lived beneath the shifting surface of the shore, waiting to rise up and grasp some unsuspecting person by the ankles and pull him or her screaming and choking down into his gritty, dry lair.

"Don't play by the lake after dark or the Sandman will get you," parents warned their children to keep them from wandering.

"Stay out of trouble or the Sandman will make you pay," teenagers joked to their friends.

Everyone supposed that it was a legend, but under the right circumstances it was a legend that could make you shiver.

One summer evening, a boy named Mark thought that he recognized the right circumstances. He was down by the lake with a girl named Jenny. The two had made a little fire and were sitting cozily beside it. It was the perfect time to tell a scary story.

"Let me tell you about the Sandman," he said, and then he told the tale with as much dramatic skill as he could muster. The effect was quite good. Although Jenny had heard the old stories before, she had never heard them told on the lakeshore, with the firelight flickering eerily and grains of sand rubbing in between her toes.

"Do you think it's true, at all?" she asked as a coyote howled in the distance.

"Who knows?" said Mark. *Who cares?* he thought. He was a boy with a limited attention span and was already thinking of other things.

"It's a good night for swimming," he declared. "Let's go in for a dip." Mark peeled off every item of clothing but his underwear and had already splashed into the lake up to his knees by the time Jenny responded.

"I don't know," she said. "It looks cold."

Mark lied to her that it wasn't chilly at all and urged her to join him. When Jenny still hesitated, he took a different approach.

"You can't stay alone on the shore," he said. "The Sandman will getcha!"

At that particular moment, the story was fresh and real in Jenny's mind. Her imagination was easily able to conjure an image of a menacing, humanoid figure rising up out of the sand beneath her feet.

"Okay, a quick swim," she agreed. She kicked off her shoes, stepped out of her blue jeans and ran out into the water.

And then she screamed. "You lied!" she shrieked at Mark. "It's freezing in here!"

Mark knew that it was, but was laughing so hard that he hardly noticed.

"Don't be mad," he said when he finally caught his breath. But Jenny was, of course.

"I'm leaving," she announced through chattering teeth, and began walking toward the shore. She was nearly there when she stopped.

"Mark," she said as she stood quite still and hugged herself for warmth. "Did you see that?"

"See what?" he said. He had begun to shiver also and was following Jenny out of the water.

"Something moved. Right in front of me, at the water's edge. The ground moved."

"Oh, right! Yeah! The Sandman!" he laughed, and continued to slosh toward the shore. "Boogedy-boogedy!" he said to Jenny when he passed her.

Mark had left his clothing scattered in a trail that led from the fire to the water. His baggy cotton pants had been the last item discarded, and so he came to them first. He reached down to pick them up.

And the ground reached up for him.

A grasping thing, like a human hand inside a sand mitten, shot up out of the shore and tried to close around his wrist. Mark was fast, though; he recoiled first and screamed second. When the writhing sand pillar closed around nothing but air, it collapsed inward. With a hollow sucking sound, it retracted into the ground, leaving only a small depression to show where it had been. Mark's pant leg was touching the outer edge of that depression, and whatever was lurking beneath the surface seemed to sense it. The hole grew a little larger; coarse grains of sand began trickling down toward its center. Then suddenly, in one lightning-swift motion, the pants were sucked downward, into the ground and out of sight.

Mark took several stumbling, splashing steps back into the lake.

"I don't believe this," he said in a voice that was tight with fear.

Jenny couldn't believe it either, but neither one of them was taking any chances. Despite the water's frigid temperature, they made no attempt to walk ashore for quite some time.

"Do you think it's gone yet?" Jenny asked 20 minutes after the pants disappeared. Her lips were turning blue and her body was becoming numb with cold.

Mark shrugged his shoulders, a gesture that looked like nothing more than another spastic shiver.

"Maybe," he said hopefully. "But I think I'll try a different part of the beach, just the same." He waded 10 yards to the left and then turned toward the shore. He was just about to step out of the water when a mound of sand swelled up to greet him.

Mark turned and ran back into the deeper water. The sand lashed out after him, like a crashing wave. Little stinging grains of it landed on his back as he made his escape.

"This isn't happening!" he screamed as he returned to Jenny's side. "The Sandman isn't real!"

"I just want to go home," Jenny sobbed. "I just want to get warm!" She stared at Mark's car, parked in the little gravel turnout just beyond the beach. It would have taken no more than two or three minutes to walk to it normally, but it might as well have been a thousand miles away. She had never been that far from the simple comforts of clothing and a car heater.

"Jen," said Mark, interrupting her thoughts, "try digging your feet into the mud."

"The what?"

"Dig your feet down into the mud at the bottom," he explained. "It's kind of warm. It feels good."

Jenny burrowed her toes into the silty bottom of the lake and felt delicious warmth trapped there.

"Oh, wow," she said as she forced her feet further down. The comfort she felt was both physical and mental. With a little bit of heat, Jenny was certain that they could last until the morning. And in her gut, she knew that nothing like the Sandman would be able to exist in the harsh light of day.

Mark was thinking the same way.

"We're going to be okay!" he said. There was such child-like relief in his voice that Jenny decided to forgive him for getting them into this horrible situation in the first place.

But it was then that she felt something tighten stealthily around the arch of her foot. When she tried to tug it free, the grip became more solid. And while her attention was focused upon that foot, she failed to notice what was happening with the other one. By the time she became aware of it, something slithery and tentacle-like had closed like a vise around her ankle.

She felt a tug, and suddenly she was choking on a mouthful of bitter lake water. When she surfaced, Mark looked at her questioningly.

"It's not mud," Jenny said as she gasped for air.

"What are you talking about?" asked Mark.

"It's not mud at the bottom of the lake," she said just before she was pulled under for the second and last time. "It's sand!"

The next day, people lined the shore by the lake while the divers recovered the bodies. Divers really hadn't been required; anybody could have walked in and pulled the blue floating corpses to shore. That was part of the mystery.

"How could two people drown," the sheriff asked the coroner, "not more than 50 feet from shore?"

The coroner couldn't say. He would only be further confused later in the day, when he performed the autopsies. For then he would wonder how two people could be found floating in lake water with their mouths packed full of dry sand.

The Vig

A young couple who had lived in this country only a short time found themselves in need of some quick money. Because they actually needed it, no bank would lend it to them. And so they considered the services of a local loan shark.

The husband's friend warned them against it.

"Don't go to Vladimir for money," he said. "He'll bleed you dry."

"Sure the interest will be high, but what else are we to do?" the husband asked. The very next day, he went looking for the man in question.

"Is Vladimir upstairs?" he asked the fat woman who ran the Russian grocery store.

She waved her hands frantically and made great shushing sounds.

"Don't be go to Vladimir," she said in her thick accent. "I'm liking you and your little wife too much." In a whisper she added, "Vladimir bleeds you dry!"

The husband shrugged.

"I have no choice," he said. "We will lose our apartment if we can't pay rent, and the bank is laughing in my face."

The woman clucked sympathetically, but there was nothing that she could do to help. Finally, with a look of great pain, she ushered the husband to a narrow staircase that was hidden behind shelves of canned sauerkraut and beets.

"You going carefully now," she begged before returning to the front of the store.

The husband walked up the creaking stairs and knocked timidly on the door at the top.

"Come in, please," said a voice on the other side. It was a deep voice, a cultured voice, not at all the type of voice that the husband expected of someone in such a seedy profession.

The husband opened the door and walked in. And he saw then that nothing about Vladimir the loan shark was what he had expected. The apartment was no dingy hideout; it was tastefully furnished and elegantly lit with candles. The polished wood and heavy velvet draperies stood out in stark contrast to the worn, gray look of the peasant grocery that was below. Downstairs, the husband had left a plain, coarse woman sorting cabbages. Upstairs, in Vladimir's quarters, he found a refined gentleman in a dinner jacket, sipping wine.

"You are Vladimir?" he asked.

The man nodded slightly to confirm.

"I am needing to do business with you," the husband said.

Vladimir nodded again, smiled and directed the husband to a beautifully upholstered wing chair.

"Sit here, please," he said, "and I will explain the terms of our contract."

Ten minutes later, the husband was mulling over the details he had just been given.

"It is unusual, I think, not to exactly define—the word, I'm not sure—'collateral.' "

Vladimir gave only a slight shrug.

"I leave it open to my interpretation. But essentially, I am only saying that if you cannot pay me on time, then I am free to take something from you. Something of my choice."

"Have you always done business this way?" the husband asked.

"Not always," came the loan shark's reply. "Things are not the way they used to be. I've had to change with the times."

The husband hesitated, but only briefly. He and his wife needed the money, so there was really no decision to be made. And he felt confident that he could keep up with the weekly rate of interest.

"I agree then," he said as he held out his hand, "and I thank you for lending us the money."

For a while, everything was alright. The husband left his weekly payments at the little Russian grocery and went about his life. But then, one week, sales were very slow at the newsstand that he operated. On top of that, there was the hardship of having to paying the dentist $50 to pull his wife's abscessed tooth. By the weekend, there was not a bit of money left over to pay Vladimir.

The wife was beside herself with worry.

"The woman at the bakery says we should never have gone to Vladimir. She says he will bleed us dry!"

"Don't worry," the husband told his wife. "He is not a thug. He will not try to take what we do not have."

But the husband's mood was grim, and as he trudged through the cold, dark streets on his way to the grocery, he had difficulty believing his own assurances.

The fat woman who sorted the vegetables would scarcely look at him when he walked through the door.

"He is being wait for you upstairs," was all she said to the husband. "Being wait to bleed you dry, da," she added to herself as he started up the stairs.

The husband found Vladimir to be just as civilized as he had been during their first visit, but not in the least bit sympathetic to his plight.

"You know my terms," the man said over and over. "You agreed to them."

Finally, the husband saw that he could do nothing except honor their contract.

"Very well," he said. "What do you want from me?"

Vladimir smiled and showed him to a comfortable-looking chaise lounge.

"Sit here," he said. "It will only take a moment." And it did.

That evening, the husband went home pale and light-headed, and praying that the following week would bring better trade to his little newsstand. When his wife opened the door of their small apartment, he nearly collapsed into her arms.

"I'll never borrow money from that Vladimir again," he gasped as he fell back on the sofa in utter exhaustion. Then he pulled away his collar to reveal two small puncture holes in the side of his neck.

"He really is going to bleed me dry," the husband said, just before his wife fainted.

Man Burger

When the sheriff called the mayor and told him that they had to meet, what he didn't have to tell him was where. It was understood that it would be their usual spot; a place that was suitably out of the way and never busy, where they could have a little privacy and the sheriff could indulge his weakness for a huge, greasy double burger with all the trimmings. They would meet, as always, at Marty's Burger Man.

Burger Man was a little roadside joint three miles outside of town. It was an old café that had sat vacant for a long time until a family from down south had taken it over, cleaned it up and started making the biggest, best burgers for miles around. The crown jewel on the Burger Man menu was the "Man Burger," two fat, sizzling meat patties layered with yellow cheese, strips of bacon and mounds of golden-fried mushrooms and onions. For a man like the sheriff, who had a seriously carnivorous streak, it was a dream come true.

"How's your cholesterol?" asked the mayor when the sheriff's order arrived. Along with the usual double burger, there was a scoop of coleslaw with an extra dollop of creamy dressing and a pile of thick-cut fried potatoes.

"Horrible," the sheriff admitted. "That's why I have to come here with you and not my wife. If she caught me with one of these burgers, she'd kill me faster than the animal fat."

"Maybe she's our culprit," the mayor whispered as he slyly raised one eyebrow.

The sheriff knew that the man was joking. Still, he winced a little at the bad taste of it. Some things weren't meant to be laughed over.

"I don't know what to do about this situation," he said around a mouthful of food. "There's another one missing now. A kid named Sherman who was living in one of those shacks over by the dump. He was doing odd jobs for people—mowed my lawn a couple of times—and now he's gone."

"So, he moved on down the line," the mayor said with a shrug.

"I don't think so." The sheriff shook his head. "He had a couple of buddies here. Didn't say anything to them. And he left all his stuff in the shack. It may look like a pile of garbage to you and me, but it was everything he had in the world and he left it behind. I know a lot of these vagrants do just pick up and go—but this one didn't. And it's time we took a good hard look at the fact that a lot of times, in this town, when a transient disappears, he's not turning up looking for handouts in the next town over."

It was the closest thing to a speech that the sheriff had ever given on the subject, mostly because the subject was taboo. For 22 months, homeless people had been vanishing from the picturesque little community where they lived. That kind of thing was bad news. Nobody wanted to see outside attention focused upon it. Especially not the mayor, the town council and various other powerful people who stood to line their pockets when the big housing developers made good on promises to turn the town into a flourishing bedroom community.

"I don't know," drawled the mayor. "Are you sure you aren't jumping to conclusions? Maybe we should wait a little while longer, just to be sure."

The sheriff used a white paper napkin to wipe a dribble of grease from his chin.

"How sure do you want me to be?" he asked. "I've got a dozen cases *that I know of*. Who knows how many loners have disappeared on their way through here? It's time to call in some feds. They've got units that specialize in this kind of situation. Serial stuff."

"Now you listen to me," the mayor said. He slid his coffee cup aside, so that he could put his elbows on the table and lean in close. "I don't want you jumping the gun here. We've waited this long, we can wait a few more months—until a few of those developers break ground. And anyway," he said, in a tone that was suddenly more light and friendly, "who's to say we really have a problem? We used to offer these bums free bus tickets to the city. Now it looks like someone might be handling the problem for us."

The sheriff was too stunned to reply—not that he had a chance. The mayor had barely finished speaking when the swinging door that led to the kitchen burst open. Through it walked the town's grocer, carrying a clipboard and wearing his usual counterfeit smile.

"Hey, hey! We've got everybody who's anybody here today!" he boomed as he strolled over to the table where the sheriff and the mayor were seated. "How you fellas doing?"

The sheriff put on his own fake-jolly face.

"How do you think I'm doing?" he laughed. "I'm busy putting away the best burger in four counties!"

"Tell me about it!" said the grocer. "Marty tries to feed me one of those every time I come out here to take his grocery order. I try to pass, though. Gotta watch my weight." He patted his stomach and put on an expression of great concern, ignoring the obvious fact that either of the men at the table would have out-weighed him by 40 or 50 pounds.

"Listen," said the sheriff, "you can tell me this. Where do you get this guy's beef? I know he's got a secret burger recipe and everything, but you can't tell me that this is the same ground beef you sell in your store."

The grocer shook his head and shrugged.

"I got no idea," he said. "He's never placed a meat order with me. Everything else, yeah. But I don't know where he gets the hamburger."

From another supplier? the sheriff wondered. It seemed unlikely, but it was the only probable answer. But the part of his mind that dealt in the improbable, the small active part that still wanted to be a real cop, told him to file the fact away. A person never knew when he might need to recall that kind of small, inter-estingly odd fact.

The grocer said that he had to head back into town then, and the mayor said that he did too. He threw a 20-dollar bill on the table, even though he had only had coffee, and left the sheriff with a wink and a closing remark.

"Be patient," he said in a low voice. "And smart. Don't disrupt any of the good things that are happening here."

The sheriff was left with his half-eaten lunch and a sour feeling in the pit of his stomach. He was staring out the window, not eating, when the proprietor of the restaurant came over to collect the mayor's coffee cup and the money for the bill.

"Sheriff, everything okay? You want me to warm that up?" He was a large, somber man who rarely spoke to his customers. The sheriff was actually a little startled by the sound of his voice.

"Marty," he said. "How long have you been open here?"

"Two years almost. Be two in January."

"And where were you before?"

"Pretty far from here. No place you'd know," the man responded. A guarded look came into his eyes.

"You know, I don't think I've ever asked you—is that your real name? Marty?" The sheriff was employing his lightest, most conversational tone of voice, but it failed to make the solemn restaurateur chatty.

"Sure," he said. "Maybe you want me to wrap that burger up then?"

The sheriff took one more look at his lunch. The food was cold and small drops of burger grease had begun to congeal on the plate. He had never before ordered a Man Burger without finishing it, but there was a first time for everything.

"No, thanks," he said. "It's time I started following my doctor's orders."

The sheriff left then, quickly, because his stomach had started to really flip-flop, and before he got out of the restaurant he didn't want to lose the part of his lunch that he had eaten. Also, he had to make a phone call to the city before he lost his courage.

☙ ☙ ☙

The sheriff had never made such a phone call without the mayor's permission before. But as with the burger he had just abandoned, there was a first time for everything.

The House of Miner

Charles Miner had always been his Uncle Howard's favorite nephew, although he lived far away. Charles's cousin Richard, on the other hand, lived under the same roof as the old man—ostensibly to provide companionship and help with upkeep of the huge Tudor-style mansion that had been in the family for nearly two centuries. Richard's physical closeness to Uncle Howard did nothing to inspire a personal bond, however. In fact, it could be fairly stated that, in that particular situation, the familiarity bred a fair amount of contempt.

When Howard Miner died, Charles was summoned from across the country to attend the small funeral and claim his large inheritance. A manservant named Tuttle, who had attended to the Miners since he had been old enough to perform the duties of a manservant, collected Charles at the airport. He delivered him first to the lawyer's office and then to the family home, where his cousin Richard welcomed him with a snifter of warm brandy.

"Sad about the old man," Richard said once they had settled in front of a fire in the parlor. "Still, he had a good long life. And he's left the two of us well enough off, which is not a bad legacy."

Charles shifted in his chair and cleared his throat self-consciously.

"Richard, about the house…" he began.

"I'm glad it's going to you," Richard said. "Uncle Howard had to choose one of us, and, after all, it is your family home, too."

"But you've lived here all these years," said Charles. "I'm worried that you feel passed over. That perhaps you have more of a claim on the place."

Richard raised the brandy bottle and looked at Charles questioningly. When Charles shook his head, Richard filled his own glass well past the point of discretion. Charles judged by his elder cousin's overflowing waistline and ruddy complexion that indulgence had become habit to him.

"The truth is, I'm a little relieved," said Richard after he had taken a good, long drink. "For years now I've been cooped up in this house with no one but our uncle and Tuttle to keep me company. I think I might like to move on now. See a bit of the world."

Charles nodded enthusiastically.

"I see your point," he agreed.

Richard heard relief in Charles's voice, which told him that Charles was less concerned about ethics than he was about how to quickly extricate a potentially stubborn tenant. Richard took a few moments to carefully consider that. When he spoke again, it was with an agenda.

"I also find myself a bit nervous here these days," he admitted. "Frankly, since Uncle Howard died, I've been fairly anxious to leave."

Charles had never known Richard to be "nervous" or "anxious" in his life. But when he looked at his cousin again, he noticed discernible tension in the set of his jaw.

"Richard," Charles said, "after all these years, why would you not be at ease in this house?"

Richard shrugged at first and seemed unwilling to elaborate. But eventually, when the silence between the men had grown too long, he glanced around the room to ensure that Tuttle was not within earshot. He leaned forward to speak to Charles in the manner of one who was sharing a tremendous confidence.

"This house has a ghost," he said in a low voice. "A banshee, to be quite specific. She is a shimmering white apparition who walks the grounds here, in wait of the day that the master of the house is to die. I have seen her many times, Charles, many times. But she was always silent. Then one night, she drifted for hours outside Uncle Howard's bedroom window, wailing inconsolably. I've never heard such keening; it nearly thinned my blood. And by that morning, the old man had passed on."

Richard drained his brandy and looked at his cousin somewhat shamefacedly.

"I know it's rather cowardly," he said, "but I don't need that kind of company. I don't need some spectral wench following me around, eager to announce my death. So, while I admit that my reasons are not the most noble, I am happy to let you be the master of this damned house."

Tuttle appeared then and interrupted the discussion with his announcement of dinner. Richard and Charles followed the butler to the dining room and sat down to a meal of venison and potatoes.

Though the subject of the ghost was not raised again, Charles found that he could not dismiss it from his mind. Richard's incessant prattling about his planned travels fell on distracted ears—for Charles believed in spirits, and therefore had to decide if he was willing to live with one.

When dinner had ended, Richard asked Charles if he might be coaxed into having another brandy.

"No, Richard, thank you," said Charles. "I believe I'll just retire. It's been a long day for me."

Richard said that he understood completely and sent his cousin off to the guest room, which had been comfortably prepared. The room had also been specially selected for its ground-level location and large window. Richard had a special plan in mind.

He intended to finish his drink and then have another. That would allow Charles ample time to fall asleep. Richard needed Charles to be sleeping, so that he could frighten him back to screaming consciousness with a carefully orchestrated simulation of the banshee. He had ghostly shrieking sounds to play on his portable tape recorder and some gauzy white cheesecloth to flutter outside the window of the guest room. Richard knew that Charles had an overactive imagination and a ridiculous fear of spirits, and he believed that it wouldn't take much more than a few theatrics to force him out of the house.

Richard hadn't lied about the banshee; she was real enough. But he had been untruthful on all other accounts; for he did want the house, he had no plan or desire to travel, and he wasn't the least bit uncomfortable about living with a wraith. On the contrary, he felt somewhat indebted to the spirit for giving him such a splendid idea. For once he had frightened Charles into refusing the house, it would automatically go to Richard.

Richard was savoring this thought, along with his second after-dinner drink, when Charles burst into the room. His breath was short, his face was chalky, and he clutched his leather suitcase, which had been so hastily repacked that a couple of shirttails and one jacket sleeve had not been tucked all the way inside.

"Charles! What on earth is the matter?" Richard was genuinely confused, as he had yet to put his plan into action.

"The banshee!" Charles gasped. "I heard her! She was moaning and wailing, just outside my bedroom window!"

"Surely you're mistaken," said Richard. "Perhaps you imagined…"

"I imagined nothing!" shouted Charles. "And what's more, I want nothing to do with this bloody haunted house! You'll have to find someone else to take it off your hands, cousin!"

With that, Charles used his own trembling hands to shred the papers he had been prepared to sign in front of the lawyer the very next day.

"I am done with it," he then told Richard. "The house is yours."

And then he was gone, leaving Richard astounded at his own good luck.

"Can you believe it?" he said to Tuttle. "Our noisy little phantom was willing to do my dirty work for me! Charles has given up the house!"

"And if he changes his mind, sir?" asked Tuttle.

Richard briefly considered that unpleasant possibility and decided that it was no real concern.

"So what if he does, Tuttle? He'll likely be dead before the lawyer's office opens. The banshee was wailing for him, after all."

"Are you quite certain, sir?" asked the somber servant. "After all, your cousin never signed the papers agreeing to take on the house. And since he has no intention of doing so, would that not make you the master?"

Richard said nothing, for he did not know how to answer. He was uncertain of how matters of ownership were determined in the spirit world.

Hours later, as he lay quaking in his bed, he knew. He knew that the banshee considered him to be the master of the house, for he had seen her brilliant white form fluttering past his window throughout the night, and he had heard her shrill cry telling him that he was doomed. By morning, the lethal combination of sheer fright and 20 years of overindulgence had stopped Richard Miner's sluggish heart.

The lawyer drafted all the paperwork that required Tuttle's signature. As the butler wrote his name again and again in his precise handwriting, the lawyer looked at him and smiled.

"Were you aware that you stood third in line to inherit the Miner house?" he asked.

Tuttle continued to write as he answered.

"No," he said. "I assure you that it was quite a surprise."

"A pleasant one, though," said the lawyer. "Quite a testament to the old man's appreciation for your years of service, I'd say. So tell me, Mr. Tuttle, what qualities do you possess, what skills do you have, that made Howard Miner think so highly of you?"

Tuttle signed his name to the last paper, leaned back and smiled.

"I believe I possess a certain tenacity, sir," he said. "A certain determination that Mr. Miner admired."

Tuttle stood up and shook the lawyer's hand, then collected his hat and put his coat over his arm. But before he walked out the door, he paused as though something else had suddenly occurred to him.

"There is one other thing that has always held me in good stead," he told the lawyer with a small smile.

"I like to air dry the linens in the fresh night breeze," he said. "The old clothesline has a terrible squeak, but it's worth it. They smell quite lovely afterward. And they look so brilliantly white."

Then, before the lawyer could comment on the odd thing the old butler had just said, he was gone, off to interview new servants to handle the many thankless chores that were required in maintaining the House of Tuttle.

Enchantment

There was once a young man who considered himself to be nearly perfect. He was tall, muscular and handsome, with wavy dark hair and eyes the color of a stormy sky. He was clever and well-spoken and destined to do very well in his career. He had many talents and many interests, and only one great problem: it was impossible to find a woman who was his match.

Repeatedly he was frustrated by what he considered to be a general lack of quality in the women he met. Some were beautiful but terribly dull. But intelligence in a woman seemed to bring with it a certain willfulness, which the man found unattractive. Then there were those with ambition and talent, who were often too self-involved to notice what a fine catch he was. No matter how determinedly social the man was, his perfect woman remained elusive. After a time, he decided to seek out professional help.

The man found himself a witch—reputed to be very powerful—and he consulted her about his problem.

"I need you to find a very special woman for me," he said. "One who is as attractive as I am and as interesting. Someone special, with whom I can have a great love affair."

The witch said little, but nodded and hummed and rocked in her old wooden chair. Eventually she

rose and shuffled into her cramped, dark little kitchen. She rummaged through the numerous boxes and bottles that littered her dusty shelves, and found several strange-looking ingredients. She ground them all into fine powder, which she then sifted into a tiny vial. She handed the vial to the man, who tried to take it without having to actually touch her rough, gnarled hands.

"Tie this to a ribbon," she instructed, "and hang it around your neck. A beautiful woman will come into your life soon."

The witch was right. The spell worked quickly. Within days, the man was going about town with a beautiful, intelligent woman on his arm.

For a while, the man believed that the witch had solved his problem. But then it became apparent that the spell was wearing thin. The woman often talked about her own interests, which bored him, and once she had the audacity to suggest that he change his hairstyle. Before long, the man was back on the doorstep of the witch's shabby little house.

"I need a better spell," he said. "Something more powerful."

The witch nodded and let him in.

On that visit, the man was forced to wait even longer in the dusty parlor while the witch created her magic. She boiled and crushed things, and said things that made no sense. She hovered over a large iron pot, carefully stirring the powerful brew that bubbled within it. Finally, she took a spoonful of the icky black dregs and put it into a small glass jar.

"Open this up once every morning," she said, "and inhale deeply from it. Your perfect woman should appear in no time."

The man did as he was told and the spell worked as it was meant to. Soon he had a new true love, who was magnificent to behold and fascinating to be with.

But unfortunately, after a week or so, the talisman began to lose its power. The man grew a little tired of seeing the same woman day after day, and his enthusiasm waned. One afternoon he told his lover he was going out for a walk. He did walk—all the way to the witch's house.

"Listen very carefully," he said once he and the witch were seated in her parlor. "I need you to use your most powerful magic. An ordinary spell won't do, for, as you can see, I am no ordinary man. Whatever it takes, whatever it costs, you must do it! Find a singular, spectacular, dynamic woman! The one woman in the world who can enchant me!"

The witch was inspired by the man's passionate plea.

"Wait here," she said, and she scurried into the kitchen. When she returned, she carried a tray with a teapot and one chipped cup.

"I will use all of my powers and all of my skills," she promised the man, "but it will take time. Have some tea while you wait."

The man sat in a lumpy old chair and drank cup after cup of cloudy bitter tea. Meanwhile, the witch took several books down from her highest shelf and began to work frantically, muttering to herself and jotting down notes. Incense was burned, strange incantations were spoken, and foul-smelling things were mixed in little clay pots. Finally, she emerged from the back rooms, looking weak and exhausted. She pushed a few damp strands of coarse, gray hair away from her sweaty brow.

"Finished your tea?" she asked the man.

He nodded.

"Good," she said, "because I have finished my spell. It is the mightiest, most creative spell that I have ever cast, but it will take some time to work. Go home now and wait. Then come back to see me in three days' time."

The man did as he was told. He went home, brimming with excitement and anticipation, and waited.

When three days had come and gone, the man knocked on the witch's door once more. When she opened it, she found him wearing his finest suit and carrying an enormous bouquet of gorgeous red roses.

"Well?" said the witch. She crossed her scrawny arms and leaned against the doorframe in anticipation of his reply.

The man was so overwhelmed by emotion that he could hardly find the words.

"I've been so blind," he said. "How could I not have seen? I've been looking for someone to worship, someone to enchant me, and all along, you were here! I shall love you forever, if you'll have me—you are so fascinating, so ravishing, so irresistibly alluring!"

"And don't forget," said the witch as she stepped aside, allowing her handsome new suitor to cross the threshold, "I also make a wicked cup of tea."

The Pirate's Ring

In a weathered little house by the sea, there once lived a man who loved to search for treasure on the sandy shore. Each morning, he would take a metal detector, a bag and a shovel and set out to see what he could find. Often there were coins. Sometimes he would uncover something more valuable, like a piece of lost jewelry. One fine day there was a money clip that still had two 20-dollar bills folded neatly in its clasp. But the finest thing he ever found, the most rare and valuable thing, was the pirate's ring. It might have made him a wealthy man, yet he never regretted what he did with it. What he did was throw it back into the water.

The man found the ring on a calm, bright morning, following a big storm. There were often interesting things littering the beach after a stormy night, so he had been highly enthusiastic when he set out on his scavenging mission.

There might be some unusual driftwood, he thought to himself. *And surely some new shells for my collection.* But the man soon forgot about such mundane items when he found the worn wooden chest.

It had been swept up into the tall grasses that grew between the water and the edge of the cliff. The man might have missed something so well-hidden had it not been very close to the path that led back to his house. He had a sharp eye, though—an eye that was accustomed to looking for things—and he noticed that one bunch of grass was bent back in an odd direction. When he looked more closely, he saw that the pale green blades were being crushed by the water-swollen little crate.

It was a sturdy thing, but rather small—the sort of box a seafaring man might once have used to securely store his valuable personal items. The lock on the front was broken and rusted, but the lid was held tightly shut by a thick leather belt that had been strapped around it. That was a bit of a mystery, for while the ornately carved chest appeared aged, the belt, with its decorative, western-style metal buckle, was obviously of a more recent era.

The man used his pocket knife to coax open the rusty buckle of the belt. Once it came loose, the chest opened easily. Inside, there was the stench of wood rot, a few small stones and one silt-encrusted treasure. The ring.

It was so filthy and black the man nearly dismissed it as another worthless rock. But it was an odd shape for a rock, so he examined it a bit more closely and scraped at it a little with his knife. Chunks of oxidation began to fall away. When it became apparent that there was heavy gold and a number of large jewels beneath the years of sediment and rust, the man could barely contain his excitement. His heart was pounding as he sat on the edge of a large flat rock, trying to rub some shine back into his newfound prize.

He was so intent upon the ring and thoughts of what price it might fetch that he didn't hear any footsteps on the path. His ears didn't pick up the whispering sounds of someone moving through the tall beach grass, and none of his senses detected the presence of someone sitting down beside him. All the same, someone did. The man was completely unaware that he had a visitor until that visitor spoke.

"That's a fine ring," he said. "It's 400 years old. Belonged to a pirate named John Clancy."

The man jumped so far that he kicked the wooden chest over and sent it rolling a short distance down the beach. He nearly dropped the ring too, but managed to snatch it out of the air before it went flying off into the loose sand. Once the ring was clutched securely in his fist, the man spun around to see who had just spoken to him. No more than three feet to his right, there sat an old man with white hair and a flowing beard to match. The old fellow wore a pleasant expression and a friendly smile, but the man was wary all the same. The man knew that the minute a person had something of value, there was another person waiting to take it away.

The visitor made no move to touch the ring, though. He didn't even ask to see it. In fact, he talked as though he had seen it a thousand times before.

"It's beautiful when it's cleaned up," he said. "That big stone in the middle is a ruby. The smaller ones, set to either side, those are diamonds. Clancy, the pirate, loved it more than any other thing he owned. I was fond of it, too, for a time. Used to wear it on my right hand. That is, until Clancy took it back. Because it's his, you know. It always will be his."

The man eyed the visitor suspiciously.

"The ring is mine," he said. "I just found it."

"It won't be yours for long," said the visitor. "That's what I'm here to tell you. Clancy will come looking for that ring and he'll take it back any way he can. And he'll take a steep price from you as well. I know. So you're better off giving it back now, before he seeks you out."

"You're crazy," said the man.

"Crazy? No," the visitor replied. "Just experienced. I thought I might save you some trouble. But I've said my piece, so I'll go now. The rest is up to you."

The mysterious visitor with the snow-white hair stood up then. He smiled as he surveyed the seashore.

"I always loved it here," he said nostalgically. I walked this beach every day."

"I've never seen you before," the man muttered. "And I've lived here a good long time."

The visitor either didn't hear the comment or chose to ignore it. Instead, he turned to the man who sat on the stone jealously guarding his treasure, and raised his hand to wave farewell.

That simple gesture was more convincing than words ever could have been. As the visitor lifted his arm, his coat parted to reveal his sturdy leather belt. A belt with a most recognizable, decorative, western-style buckle.

The man had been about to mention the coincidence when his eye was drawn to the visitor's raised hand. What he saw shocked him into silence. He looked away for a moment, to the precious, heavy ring that sat in the palm of his own hand. Right then and there he decided that he would not keep it.

The man looked up again, wanting to tell the visitor of his decision, but the visitor was gone. As silently as he had appeared, he had vanished. And somehow, the man was not surprised.

That very morning, even before he went back to his little house, the man returned the pirate's ring to its wooden chest. Then, with the belt strapped tightly around it once more, he returned the chest to the sea. It was thrown from high atop a cliff and weighted with heavier stones than before, in the hope that it would stay far from shore and not be a temptation to someone else. For though the ruby and diamonds were likely worth a small fortune, they were not worth the price of angering the ghostly pirate Clancy.

The visitor who had come to warn the man had known that. And he had been missing the third finger—the ring finger—of his weathered right hand.

Black Aggie

It was a lovely, warm Friday night. A group of teenagers were enjoying it in the unlikeliest of places: the local cemetery. There were four of them—two girls and two boys—lying on a freshly mown grassy slope, watching the stars wink into existence as the sky grew dark. One of the fellows, a boy named Ethan, glanced at his watch often. He felt wonderfully content with the soft warm breeze on his face and his friends around him, but he still didn't want to get caught in the cemetery after midnight.

"Let's go," he finally said. "It's getting late."

But Ethan's friends didn't want to go. They were comfortable where they were and in the midst of a deep philosophical conversation.

"I want to stay," said one of the girls. "This place is great."

She was right. Ethan had often thought that cemeteries were wasted on the dead, on those who no longer possessed the senses necessary to take in the beauty and tranquillity that surrounded them. But there were some things that weren't worth any amount of atmospheric pleasure, and spending a night with Black Aggie was one of them.

Black Aggie was a life-sized marble statue that marked a grave in the shadowy center of the cemetery. The female form had been seated there for decades, with her arms held out before her. Her stone robes draped gracefully around her and her hair was gently upswept. Aggie had the benign face of an angel, but the reputation of a demon.

"It's her eyes," Ethan said to his friends as he told them the story. Black Aggie had the pale, blank, staring eyes of a statue by day. But it was said that in the darkest hours of the night they glowed fiercely red.

Josh, the other boy in the group, nearly choked on his soda when he heard that.

"A statue who gives you the evil red eye? Oh, come on! You don't believe that?" he said.

Ethan felt his cheeks grow warm.

"It's not just an evil eye," he insisted. "I've heard that if you look directly at her, you'll go blind. And what's more, she's more dangerous to guys. She hates guys. Because of how she died."

The girls were curious then. They had to know how it was that Aggie's life had ended. Ethan told them the story that his mother had told him, that Aggie had been left at the altar by a cheating fiancé and had died of a broken heart.

This sent Josh into hysterics.

"I can't believe you're so gullible!" he gasped when he had finally finished laughing. "That's what they call 'a legend,' Ethan. Or 'an old wives' tale.' But I gotta admit, I want to see that statue now." And then Josh said that he would be willing to find another place to spend the evening, as long as they could visit Black Aggie on the way out of the cemetery.

Ethan hesitated. It was very late and very dark. He was no longer comfortable being in the cemetery, let alone right beside the statue. But if paying a brief visit to the notorious marble woman was what it would take to get everyone moving along, that's what they would do.

"Okay," he said. "This way."

The four teens picked themselves up off the ground and started down the gentle hill that led into the dark center of the cemetery. It was the oldest part, the original burial ground, and the tombstones sat beneath the protective branches of many massive, ancient-looking trees. Black Aggie sat in the shadow of one particularly large oak. Her lap was filled with leaves and debris that had fallen from above.

"Is this it?" Josh asked when they had gathered around her. "Is this Evil Aggie?"

Ethan nodded. "So, now you've seen her. Now we can go," he urged.

But Josh wasn't finished having his fun. He poked and prodded at the statue, daring her to do her worst. Then he draped one arm around her cold shoulders and expressed his insincere sympathy for her sad situation. "So many men to blind—so little time," he quipped.

It was all making Ethan terribly nervous.

"You wanted to see her on the way out," he said. "So, let's go now. Let's find something else to do."

Josh was about to comply when he recognized a fine opportunity to frighten Ethan and impress the girls in one smooth action.

"You go," he said slyly. "I'm going to stay here and visit Aggie for a while." And with that, he climbed up onto the base of the statue and seated himself in her lap. He leaned comfortably back against one of the marble woman's outstretched arms and dangled his legs over the other.

Ethan and the two girls provided a background chorus of gasps.

"You can't do that!" said one of the girls. "It's disrespectful!"

"Totally inappropriate," said the other.

Ethan looked less outraged, but more purely frightened.

"Josh," he begged. "Get down. Let's go. I mean it."

But Josh was put out that the girls hadn't shown the proper appreciation for his daring. He lowered his eyes and stuck his lip out in a stubborn pout.

"You go," he said. "You can *all* go. I don't feel like hanging out anymore."

And so, the three teens left their friend sitting in the lap of the stone statue with the bad reputation. They walked out of the cemetery and went their separate ways because, somehow, the fun had gone out of the evening.

Early the next morning, Ethan received a phone call from one of the girls.

"Josh's mom just called me," she said in a frightened voice. "She's looking for him. She said he didn't come home last night."

"He's just trying to freak everyone out," said Ethan. He said it to be reassuring, but there was a churning in the pit of his stomach that told him that he didn't believe it himself. Of course, there was only one way to know for sure.

An hour later, Ethan met the girls at the entrance to the cemetery. There were no greetings and there was no small talk. Once they had gathered, they began to walk down the path that led into the tree-lined, shadowy center of the burial ground.

"I bet he's waiting for us," said one of the girls. "He knows we'd come looking for him."

"This is all a big joke to him," said the other.

Ethan said nothing until the threesome rounded the corner and Black Aggie came into full view.

"There he is," he said then as the girls both sighed with relief. They could all see Josh, still resting comfortably in the statue's lap. His head lay peacefully on the marble woman's shoulder.

"He fell asleep," said one of the girls. Ethan and the other girl nodded in agreement, but Ethan noted that his stomach was still revving in high gear.

"Josh!" he shouted. "Wake up!"

There was no answer.

"Josh, this isn't funny!" one of the girls screamed.

But the boy remained as still as the statue itself. It was only when they were close enough to touch him that he began to stir.

"Is that you guys?" he said in a voice that was small and weak and unlike the Josh they knew.

"It's us," said Ethan. "Why didn't you go home last night?"

Josh turned to them then and showed his face, and before he said anything they knew the answer.

"I couldn't find my way…" he began as he looked at them with eyes that were as smooth and blank and hauntingly white as the statue's. "And she wouldn't let me go," he finished as he held up his arm for inspection.

The girls turned away, but Ethan couldn't stop staring. There, on Josh's biceps, which had been resting in Black Aggie's open hand, were the deepest, blackest bruises Ethan had ever seen.

They were, of course, in the shapes of five stone fingers.

The Lost Lights

"…and from that day forward, the campers shivered in their tents any time they heard the howl of the ghostly black hound."

There were five young boys sitting in a semicircle around the campfire. They all stared at the storyteller with wide, wonder-filled eyes.

"Is that true, Uncle Frank?" asked the youngest of the group. "Did that really happen around here?"

Frank Carson nodded solemnly.

"I swear that it did. Would I tell you a story if it wasn't true?"

There was a cynical snort of laughter from the oldest of the boys, a 12-year-old who was Frank's own son.

"They're all tall tales, Dad—but they're good ones. Can you tell us one more?"

The other boys instantly added their own pleas for just one more story. They had an unquenchable thirst for Frank's well-told tales and looked deeply disappointed when he shook his head.

"Nah, it's real late," he said. "We had a long hike today and it's time to hit the ol' bedroll."

There was a bit of grumbling, but only a bit. The boys had spent two long hours that afternoon packing their gear into the remote little campsite. They had spent another hour setting up camp. They loved being on their annual wilderness excursion, but they were bone-tired. Also, they knew that they would be spending the next evening sitting around the fire, too, and that Frank would be good for at least two or three more spooky stories then.

" 'Night, boys." Frank gave each kid a good-natured pat on the shoulder as they filed past him, one by one, before disappearing into the two large tents. There was a bit of rustling about, a few minutes of Frank watching the boys' shadows bob here and there on the canvas walls. Then the flashlights were turned off and everyone grew quiet. Within minutes, the sound of soft snoring could be heard. Frank smiled and stirred the ashes of the fire. It was his time then, time to be alone with his thoughts in the quietest part of the world that he knew.

The Carsons spent a week before school every fall surrounded by that quiet, natural beauty. Frank would bring his family and his sister would bring hers, and they would all meet at the rustic lodge that sat just outside of the wilderness preserve. For a couple of days, everyone socialized and enjoyed the reunion. Then Frank would round up all the boys and set out on a two-day excursion into the wilds. It was good for kids, he thought, to get away from their television sets and video games for a while and see what a lake looked like when it was still untouched by jet-skis. He knew that it was good for him. He loved to spend time listening to the natural sounds of the night and looking at the stars in a place where they weren't outshone by neon and street lamps.

For a while, he sat there in the dark and watched the embers die. But Frank had been the one to haul most of the camping gear up the winding, rocky trail, and it wasn't long before his eyes refused to stay open.

"Tomorrow's another day," he said quietly to himself as he stood up and stretched. He was looking forward to the morning, thinking about the activities he had planned for the boys, when a mysterious sight captured his attention.

Shooting star? he wondered, and squinted into the distance. But when he caught sight of it again he knew that it wasn't. It was a tiny ball of yellow light, bobbing slowly around the perimeter of the low, rugged mountains that bordered the opposite shore of the lake.

Frank rubbed at his tired eyes and took a deep breath. When he looked up again, the light had vanished. Before there was even time for a sense of relief to set in, though, the light was back and it had company. Two minute, glowing orbs bounced unevenly along the mountainside. It was an unsettling sight. Frank forgot about crawling into a warm sleeping bag. Instead, he reached for his backpack and fished out a pair of binoculars.

An hour later, there were six of them and Frank was scared. Not worried or concerned, but scared. Scared enough to rouse the boys from their deep sleeps.

"C'mon," he said softly. "Everybody's gotta get up. There's a little change of plans."

There were many groggy complaints, but the boys did as they were told. They came out of their sleeping bags and out of their tents and stood shivering in front of the cold ashes of the fire.

"What's going on?" Frank's son asked sleepily.

Frank pulled out the gear packs and began to dismantle one of the tents as he replied.

"Nothin' too much," he said, and he hoped that his voice didn't betray either his fear or his lie. "I'm sensing that we might get a little weather. Some rain. So I thought that instead of being cold and wet out here, we should get back to the lodge and have a roof over our heads."

The boys stared skyward, then looked at each other in confusion.

"There aren't any clouds," said one.

"There's no wind," said another.

"Dad, it's a two-hour hike. It might even take three, in the middle of the night."

Everything that the boys were saying was true, but Frank didn't have time for a debate. He needed them to get dressed, get packed and move out. And everything would go more smoothly if they weren't frightened. So Frank did what he had to do. He looked the five youngsters squarely in the eyes and bribed them.

"You guys get moving right now," he said, "and while we're on the trail, I'll tell you one of the best ghost stories you ever heard. It's from here and it's true. I promise."

It was the nudge that they needed. Within 15 minutes, both tents were down and the supplies had been repacked. Five minutes after that, with Frank and the two oldest boys wielding powerful flashlights, the campers started out on their midnight trek.

"Tell us that story now. The really good one," Frank's youngest nephew begged once the group had hit its stride.

Frank cleared his throat. He was falling-down tired and leading a group of equally exhausted boys on a very long walk. He had to make them move, without making them afraid. That called for extreme distraction, which meant that he had to be the most entertaining that he had ever been in his life. Frank wasn't entirely sure that he could manage it, but he dove in bravely.

"It all happened more than 200 years ago," he began, "to a party of settlers who were traveling through here on their way to the west coast. There were two families, they say, who had banded together to make the hard journey. Unfortunately, not one of those people knew of a good path to take through the mountains. They eventually decided to pass through here, on the north side of the lake."

"But that's dangerous!" one of the boys said. "Didn't they know how steep and rocky that is?"

Frank smiled. His repeated lectures about never wandering around to the mountainous side of the small lake had not fallen on deaf ears after all.

"No, they didn't know," he said. "They had no one to tell them. So there they were, trying to negotiate paths so slippery and narrow that even the mountain goats steered clear of them. They had little kids to hang on to and heavy packs to carry and the horses were so skittish that they had to blindfold 'em and lead 'em along the trail, step by step. Their situation was plenty bad and about to get worse.

"It was late in the fall and the weather was growing cool. The settlers had wrapped themselves in a few layers of warm clothing, but they weren't really prepared for winter conditions. After all, they were sure that they would be happily set up beside the Pacific Ocean before the snow flew. But there was another thing that they didn't know about these mountains: the way the weather could change so quickly. And as they were inching their way along the path, trying to not fall into the freezing lake, a storm was blowing in.

"It wasn't just any storm. It was one of those wicked blizzards that only seem to brew really early in the season or really late. The kind where the wind whips tiny icicles at your face and you can't see a person who's standing more'n 10 feet away. They didn't know it until it was too late, of course. They were halfway 'round the mountain by the time the sky had gone dark and the wind had started to gust. They couldn't stay where they were then; most spots on that path there isn't even room to sit yourself comfortably down, let alone build a fire and a shelter and bed down for the night. So they just kept going and they prayed that the weather would let up."

"And did it?" one of the younger boys interrupted Frank. The other four simultaneously shushed him.

"You hafta wait and find out in the story," one said. Frank was pleased. He knew then that the boys were caught up in the tale and not thinking about their weariness or their sore feet.

"The storm didn't let up," Frank continued. "In fact, it went on for hours. The snow was blowing so furiously around the settlers that they were blinded by it. They were literally feeling their way around that mountain. Eventually, they grew so afraid of taking a wrong step on the trail that they slowed to a dead stop. They just clung to the face of the rock, feeling their hands and feet go numb while the ice and snow found its way down their collars and up their sleeves. The men and women who were leading the group knew that every one of them was going to freeze if they didn't do something. So they did something.

"They took out their lanterns," Frank said solemnly. "It may not sound like a daring thing, or a brave thing, but it was. Just standing still was precarious enough at that point; digging through the saddlebags on skittery horses was like walking a tightrope. The other thing was that they had so little kerosene. They had been conserving it for weeks. Matches were in short supply, too, but they unpacked them just the same. And each time they jostled those supplies around, they risked sending either themselves or the packs that held their means of survival down into the lake.

"Well, the wind was howling and the snow was blowing and it took quite a few tries to get even one lantern wick lit. But they did it, and then they lit another and another and another. They lit every lantern that they had with them and passed them carefully down the line. Once the lights were spread out, each of them could see a little bit better. Plus, they had something to follow. They could tell when there was a dip or a bend coming up. The terrain was just as dangerous, but it couldn't surprise them so much.

"But maybe that was part of the problem, in the end; the fact that each person was almost hypnotically following the lamp that was in front of him. Because the group eventually came to this little slope that had gotten real slick with ice. The fellow that was leading, he started edging down the path, real slow and easy, but he still lost his footing. He slipped and he fell, straight down into the lake. He took his lantern with him, and his whole family watched in horror as that light disappeared over the side of the precipice. They say that quite a few of them leaned over to keep the light in their sights, and that they lost their balance and fell, too. Fell screaming, still clutching their lanterns, all the way into the cold, black water.

"By the time the storm had ended and the group had made it through the treacherous mountain pass, they were missing more than half their number. And they say that the ones who perished along the way occasionally relive their terrifying final hours. People know, because every so often they see the glow of their lanterns. These little pinpoints of light move unsteadily and ever so slowly along the base of the mountain. They call them the 'lost lights,' because they are the lost souls of the settlers who never made it through the storm."

There were a few moments of respectful silence. Then Frank's son spoke.

"Wow, Dad," he breathed. "Did that really happen, right here?"

"You can look it up when we get back to the lodge," said Frank. "I'm pretty sure the part about the settlers and the storm is in a local history book. The part about the 'lost lights,' well, you just have to take my word on that."

"Have you ever seen them?" the boy asked.

Frank paused for just a second before he answered.

"Just once," was all he said.

Frank and the boys made it back to the lodge in good time considering that they were walking in the dark and badly in need of rest. It was still the wee hours of the morning when they crested the hill that took them out of the woods and into the open pasture where the lodge was situated.

Because of the time, they were surprised to see lights blazing and a group of people bustling about on the building's main veranda. When they grew closer, Frank could see men loading survival gear onto the backs of a couple all-terrain vehicles.

"What's going on?" he called out when he was close enough to be heard. At the sound of his voice, every one of the people turned and squinted into the darkness.

"It's them!" somebody shouted as Frank and the boys came walking into the illumination of the powerful yard lights. There was an eruption of excited comments from the crowd. Then Frank's sister and his wife pushed their way through the group and came running across the lawn to meet him.

"Thank goodness, thank goodness," his wife said over and over. Her face showed evidence of some great strain. Frank glanced at his sister and noted that there was worry and tension etched in her features as well.

"What's going on?" he said, this time to his wife.

She told him that there was a storm blowing in, a freak, early-season storm that was likely to be the

worst in decades. They had been told to expect freezing rain, followed by a blizzard. Temperatures were
supposed to drop more than 20 degrees overnight.
Campers from all over the area were being rounded
up and brought in to safety.

"But you and the boys were the farthest out," she
said, "and the bad weather is coming from that direction. It's supposed to hit the lake first. In fact, it's
probably already there. So they sent a search and res-
cue team," she explained as she pointed to the men by
the loaded ATVs.

Frank's wife sighed with relief once more. Then
she paused as a question occurred to her.

"It's the middle of the night," she said to him.
"How did you know that you had to come back?"

It was Frank's turn to pause then. He took his wife's
arm and moved a few steps away from the others.

"I saw the 'lost lights,' " he said in a quiet voice.

Frank's wife went pale, for she knew the legend,
too—including a part of it that he had not seen fit to
share with the boys.

It had long been believed that when the lost lights
appeared, it was to serve as a dire warning. Those
souls who had perished in the mountain lake more
than two centuries before showed their lanterns for
only one reason: to signal that a vicious, deadly storm
was on its way.

"How many?" Frank's wife asked him. When he

responded by holding up all the fingers of his right hand, plus his left thumb, her hand flew to her mouth in an expression of horror.

"All of you!" she gasped, and he nodded.

Frank began to shake a little then, as the reality of what had nearly happened began to sink in. For it was true what the legend said about how the spirits always personalized the omen.

They did it by showing one lantern…for every person who was about to die.

The Best House on the Block

Every Halloween there was one family in one particular neighborhood who would go to great lengths in decorating their house. Their goal was always the same: to create a wonderfully frightening atmosphere for all the trick-or-treaters. The neighborhood children loved it—even though the younger ones sometimes found that when October 31st arrived, they were too nervous to actually walk up to the front door and collect their candy.

The people who lived on the street loved it, too—even though some of them felt that their own little jack-o-lanterns and cardboard cutouts of witches and skeletons didn't receive enough flattering attention in comparison. A few of the more competitive types would take a look at what the family created and vow that the following year they would outdo them. But nobody ever did. That family always had the best house on the block.

It was well known that they loved the attention. At least they did until the one year when they got more attention than any of them had bargained for. By the time it was over, pictures of the spookily decorated front yard had been on the front page of the paper and even on the six o'clock news.

They had created a haunted cemetery that year. Plywood tombstones jutted out of the front lawn at creepy, random angles, and a rickety fence had been erected, with jaggedly broken pickets that stabbed skyward. There were strands of sticky cobwebs lacing over the archway that led to the yard, and gruesome props splashed in red-colored corn syrup had been set everywhere. The two teenaged daughters dressed up in ghoulish costumes and loitered menacingly beside the path. And anyone who was brave enough to pass them had yet one more fright in store before they reached the front door. A coffin, designed to look freshly unearthed, had been placed at the base of the porch steps. The lid was cracked open just a little. It was enough to make a person nervous, and rightly so—for those who were bold enough to walk directly in front of it risked having a corpse-like hand reach out to grasp their ankles. It was a terrifically scary effect.

Still, there were those who clucked their tongues and said that on that particular Halloween it was all in very bad taste. For that was the year of "The Body Snatcher," as the local media had dubbed him.

The Body Snatcher was a criminal with a particularly ghoulish modus operandi. He would dig up freshly buried coffins and steal the bodies that had been laid to rest within them. Thoughtful fellow that he was, though, he never left a casket empty. He would always replace the corpse that he had stolen with a freshly slain animal; a stray cat, usually, or sometimes a bird. The authorities were greatly concerned that The Body Snatcher would be inspired to strike yet again on Halloween night, and security had been tightened at all the local cemeteries.

Of course the family hadn't been thinking about the horrible headlines; they only wanted to create the best Halloween display ever. It was in that spirit that they had designed the cemetery and fashioned the fake coffin and then decided that the brother—who was the eldest and the one who achieved the greatest pleasure out of scaring people—would be the one to hide inside it.

Halloween was a moonless night, but the torches placed about the yard cast long, flickering shadows. Groups of children fueled by massive doses of sugar summoned up every ounce of their bravado in order to pass through the staged cemetery. There were shrieks and howls, and the genuine screams of some who didn't make it. Often a mere tap on the shoulder by one of the costumed sisters was enough to send someone leaping into the air or bounding back down the path to the safety of the front street. More often, though, the trick-or-treaters went all the way to the door, where the brother would snake his arm out of the partially opened coffin and clutch at their pant legs. It was all so exciting, so very entertaining, that nearly everyone of every age was delighted.

Only Mr. Cross, the nasty taxidermist from the house next door, remained unamused.

"It's in terrible taste," he complained to the parents. "It's a mockery of the very serious things that are going on."

Everyone knew that Mr. Cross was just put out because no one had ever made such a fuss over the genuine stuffed bat that he always hung near his door for Halloween. But of course the parents didn't say that. Instead, they nicely explained that there was no disrespect intended, and besides, weren't the children all having a very good time and wasn't that the main thing?

Mr. Cross sniffed the air and left. He took to loitering near the fence that marked the property line between the two houses, where, presumably, he could keep a running list of all of the evening's offenses.

About nine o'clock there was a lull. The younger children had all lugged their heavy bags of candy home by then. The older ones, who would be guests at the family's Halloween party, were not scheduled to arrive yet. The sisters, who were sweating and uncomfortable inside their elaborate costumes, decided to take a break.

"Are you coming in for a bit of a rest?" they asked their brother in the coffin.

"I'm staying here," he replied. "The guys will be showing up any time, and I don't want to miss the chance to make them scream."

So the brother stayed in the coffin and the sisters took a break. Half an hour later, when the girls returned to their posts, they noticed that Mr. Cross had abandoned his surveillance.

They had less fun with the older kids, the party guests. Teenagers were harder to frighten and much less likely to admit it even if they *were* frightened. The sisters began to lose interest in their roles and saw that their brother had as well. He hadn't bothered to grab a single ankle since the girls had come back outside.

But when the girls saw two tall dark creatures approaching, they knew that their brother's interest was about to be revived. Despite the hoods and the masks, they recognized their brother's best friends, the ones he had been waiting all evening to scare.

The two boys were good sports with the sisters. They pretended to be at least surprised, if not frightened. The girls laughed and told them to go on to the house and then held their breath as the guys approached the front door.

Nothing happened.

The boys walked up the porch steps and into the house without incident. The girls' brother hadn't moved. Something had to be wrong.

The sisters ran over to the coffin and flipped it open. Their brother wasn't there; there was no sign of him. In his place, there was a dead and bloody raven.

The girls began to scream.

For a time, it was thought that the brother had played the ultimate Halloween prank on his own family, allowing them to think that he had been taken by The Body Snatcher. But days passed and he didn't return home, and it was eventually accepted that he was the most gruesome statistic in the police's Body Snatcher case file. That was a case file that remained unsolved for one more full year.

The next Halloween no one expected the family to put on their usual dramatic show and, of course, they didn't. Even the other homes in the neighborhood were decorated with less enthusiasm than usual. It was silently agreed upon that decorating for Halloween would not have been in good taste.

Mr. Cross, however, who had been so very concerned with good taste the previous year, seemed nearly giddy as he made his preparations. For a week before, he was outdoors with a stepladder, hanging strings of dull orange lights and stapling wispy bits of synthetic cobweb to his overgrown pine trees. He hung the famous bat just above his entranceway, and in an act of truly tactless decorating, propped an empty, open casket just below it.

"That's terrible!" whispered Mrs. Pike, who lived across the street, to one of the other neighbors. "He couldn't have done anything worse."

But on Halloween night, she was proved wrong.

On Halloween night, the first trick-or-treaters to approach Mr. Cross's door ran screaming back into the arms of their parents. Those same parents ran home, locked their doors and called the police.

When the police arrived, they found Mr. Cross sitting on his front porch, holding a bowl of candy and beaming broadly. The casket, propped up against the porch railing, was no longer empty. It held the taxidermically preserved body of the neighbor family's missing son.

"He was much fresher than all the others," boasted The Body Snatcher. "It all worked out much better."

"And now," he added as he leaned forward and delivered a sly wink, "now who has the best house on the block?"

Part Three
Stories told by Candlelight

*In certain intimate circumstances, it becomes clear
that each one of us has our own tale to tell.
When we switch off the electricity and whisper
with one another beside the wavering yellow flame
of a melting candle, those stories emerge.*

*They can be curious, mystifying and even terrifying.
Always, they are original and unique.
They are the stories told by candlelight…*

The Rope

During the Great Depression, in a one-room rural schoolhouse, there was a particularly rambunctious student named Jack. Jack wasn't bad; even his teacher had to admit to that. He was just curious and "full of the dickens," as they used to say. His energetic nature often landed him in trouble and he was accustomed to taking a lick of punishment. But the worst trouble that Jack ever got into, and the longest punishment that he ever endured, was over something that was never even his fault.

The schoolhouse had a playground—but it wasn't a playground by today's marvelous standards. It was a little clearing with a place where the kids could run races or play stickball, if anyone was so fortunate as to have a ball. Off to the side, there was a big old tree with a strong branch that jutted out at an angle. There was a sturdy length of rope that had been thrown over that branch and tied to a smoothly worn wooden plank. It made a fine swing—the closest thing to "playground equipment" that anybody had in those days.

Jack's trouble started on the morning when that rope went missing. The teacher assumed that one of the children had stolen it as a prank. More specifically, she assumed that it had been Jack.

"Miss, I swear, I didn't touch it," Jack said when he was accused. Unfortunately, the circumstantial evidence weighed heavily against him.

"The other boys are too young and too small to get into such mischief," said the teacher, "and the girls would never do such a thing. Also, I noticed that you arrived early this morning, Jack, which is unlike you."

Had Jack not been a big boy of 12, he would have cried at the injustice of it. Only the week before, he had been punished for tardiness. Now it appeared that punctuality would be his undoing.

"What's my punishment?" he asked when it became obvious that there was no point in continuing the debate.

The teacher crossed her arms and put on her most stern expression.

"You will do the chores here every day until that rope is returned," she decreed. "That means hauling in the wood and the coal and emptying the ash pan. Before you leave at the end of the day, you will make certain that the floors are swept and the blackboard is clean. I hope this proves to you, Jack, that I won't be lenient where a matter as serious as stealing is concerned."

Jack was devastated. Punishment was one matter, but endless punishment was another altogether. Since he hadn't taken the rope and didn't know where the rope was, he had no way of returning it. He spent the remainder of the day feeling very sorry for himself indeed.

As Jack lay in bed that night, he found himself tossing and turning. The events of the day and his seemingly unsolvable problem were weighing heavily on his mind. When, finally, he did drift into unconsciousness, he found no peace waiting for him there either. Instead, Jack was drawn into one of the most vivid and terrible nightmares that he had ever had.

He dreamed that he heard the rough wooden planks of his bedroom floor creaking. Jack turned to see who was walking through his tiny room in the middle of the night. He had expected to see one of his sisters, or perhaps his father, on the way to the outdoor privy. He had not been prepared to see a terrifying hobo lurching across the room toward him.

He was a tall, scrawny, unshaven man with a shock of filthy wild hair. His eyes were darkly circled and appeared huge within his skull-like face. Layers of tattered clothing hung from his bony frame. But what Jack would later remember most about the nightmare was the way the hobo had appeared to be reaching out in a horribly menacing pose. Stretched tautly between one chapped, dirty fist and the other had been a good length of sturdy rope.

The next day, the teacher asked Jack if he was sorry yet.

"I'm near the sorriest I've ever been," he told her truthfully. But because he could not produce the swing rope, he was forced to do the chores. At the end of the day, when he carried in the last pile of cordwood, his teacher looked at him and shook her head sorrowfully.

"You may be the most stubborn boy I have ever known," she said.

There was no reply that Jack could think of, so he simply nodded and went home.

That night the hobo was in his dreams again.

Jack pulled his thin quilt up to his nose when he saw the ominous skeletal figure crossing his bedroom floor.

"Leave me alone!" he shouted in his dream. But the loathsome character continued to approach and extended his arms toward Jack, with the hank of rope still clutched tightly in his grimy hands.

The next morning, as she spooned out his share of oatmeal, Jack's mother asked him what on earth he had been going on about during the night.

"Bad dream," he mumbled. Indeed, the boy was starting to look as though he was suffering from a lack of rest. That day, even his teacher took note of the dark circles beneath his eyes and the general pallor of his complexion. At noontime, when the other children had gone outdoors to play, she took pity on Jack.

"I'm disappointed that you haven't yet returned the rope," she lectured, "but you have been good to do so many chores without a word of complaint. When you finish cleaning the ash box, you may go outside for some fresh air."

162 Campfire Ghost Stories

"Thank you, miss," Jack said, and he finished his task in record time.

Jack felt hopeful for the first time in days. He had been granted a bit of free time and his teacher was showing signs of softening on the issue of eternal punishment. No sooner had he stepped out of the schoolhouse and into the sunshine, though, than his upbeat mood was shattered.

Two of the younger children came running out of the dense woods that surrounded the clearing, shrieking as though they were being chased by the devil.

"There's a man!" one of them screamed.

"A man in the trees!" wailed the other.

The great commotion that they made drew the teacher outdoors and the other children away from their games. The small crowd gathered around the steps of the schoolhouse as the two terrified little boys blurted out their story.

"We was explorin', " said one.

"But not too far," added the other, remembering that the teacher had strict rules about leaving the clearing.

"We found a man," they said together. After a few moments of their vivid description, it became obvious that the boys had come across not just a man, but a dead man. There was a corpse in the woods and someone needed to investigate.

The teacher sent the younger children into the school. Then she told the older girls to go in and watch over the little ones. Then she was left standing on the steps with Jack. He was the oldest boy in the class, the biggest and the strongest.

"Will you come to help me?" she asked him.

"Yes, miss," he nodded, and the two started off toward where the two children had emerged from the trees.

The little boys hadn't been lying. They truly hadn't gone too far beyond the clearing. Jack and the teacher had taken only a few steps into the tangled underbrush themselves when they saw a shabby-looking pair of boots dangling in front of them. When they pulled a mass of leafy branches aside, they were able to see the man who was wearing the boots.

Jack sucked his breath in sharply. Despite the odd tilt of his head and the slightly protruding black tongue, the dead fellow was instantly recognizable. It was the menacing hobo of Jack's nightmares.

Then, suddenly, the teacher told Jack that she was so very sorry.

How could she know about my dream? he wondered. But as he looked skyward, he realized why she was apologizing.

The hobo had hanged himself with the rope stolen from the tree swing.

* * *

That night Jack dreamed of the hobo one last time. It was a different dream, though, because it was much less disturbing and because the dead man spoke. It began, as it had the other times, with the familiar creaking of the wooden floor. When Jack rolled over and opened his eyes, he saw the poor hobo again. But this time, the man seemed less desperate and he wasn't advancing on Jack with the rope. In fact, the rope wasn't even in his hands.

When Jack saw that, he looked at the hobo with a questioning expression. The man smiled sadly and nodded.

"I was just trying to give it back, kid," he said in a voice that was somehow tinny and hollow all at the same time. "I never meant to getcha in trouble."

He vanished then, leaving Jack alone with his overwhelming sense of relief.

He didn't need a fellow like that around. Jack managed to get into enough trouble all on his own.

The Calling Woman

There once was a hardworking trapper whose wife was a terrible vexation to him. She routinely spent more money than what the couple had, complained about every little thing and nagged at her husband both night and day.

"You can't be trusted to do a thing right," she often told the trapper, and he seldom argued in his own defense. The poor man had learned early in their marriage that to do so was a foolish waste of time.

Instead, the trapper counted his few blessings, not the least of which was that he spent many blissful hours alone when he went into the wilderness to tend to his trap lines. There came a terrible day, however, when the wife decided that she should accompany the trapper on one of his trips.

"I want to see that you're not wasting time up there," said the wife. "How do I know that you couldn't be working harder and earning us a better living? We'll go out to the cabin together this time, so I can keep my eye on you."

The trapper was dismayed but said nothing. He simply hoped that the rough state of the isolated little cabin and the cold, bleak wilderness conditions would be sufficient to discourage her from staying.

He was ultimately disappointed.

The wife did complain bitterly about her rustic surroundings, but she also made it clear that she was staying.

"This is what you come to when I'm not around," she harped, "slovenly conditions and lazy ways." Then she rattled off a list of chores for her husband to attend to.

"I have a trap line to set!" he protested. But he received no sympathy or understanding.

"You can't work the trap line after the sun's gone down," the wife stated. "So that's when you can see to the cleaning and repairs around the cabin."

The trapper toyed with the notion of saying "And when shall I sleep?" In the end, however, he thought that showing a smart tongue would only serve to bring more work raining down upon him.

For several days the trapper labored. When morning came, he went out on his trap line. In the evening, he dealt with some chore around the cabin. He sorely missed the days when he could work unsupervised, take his leisure in front of a roaring fire and sleep until he was ready to rise.

Happily, there came one day when the trapper had to venture out to tend to the most remote portion of the line. It meant several hours of travel and necessitated camping overnight. The man had never looked quite so forward to sleeping on the cold, hard ground.

"Stay close to the cabin," he told his wife before he left. "This bush is wild and thick, and you could easily get lost."

The wife took the warning as an insult.

"I can care for myself far better than you can," she snapped back. "I guarantee you, I'll do as I like."

The trapper looked at his wife then, with her firmly set jaw and her mean eyes, and he recognized an opportunity. Knowing that she was contrary enough to defy him on principle, he warned her one more time.

"Stay in the cabin, woman!" he demanded. "The deep woods is no place for someone as helpless as you. If you must go out, keep the cabin well in sight! Never, *ever* go wandering off!"

He turned quickly then and left. The last sight he had of his ill-tempered wife's face showed her features twisting into an expression of furious defiance. It was an image that would stay with him for a very long time.

The trapper went away for two days and two nights. During the long hike back to the cabin, he could not help noticing the tiny tingle of anticipation that was stirring in his stomach.

"Hello!" he called out when the cabin came into sight. But his wife did not answer.

"Hello!" he said again as he threw open the door. But his wife was not inside.

"Hello, hello!" he chuckled to himself as he felt the cold grate of the fireplace and saw that no lunch had been laid out upon the table. It was obvious that his wife was gone. She had wandered into the wilderness to defy him and had gotten herself lost.

The trapper, feeling giddy and free, set about making himself a little meal. He opened a tin of beans and sliced up a generous portion of salt pork. As he built a fire to warm himself and the food, however, he suffered a terrible shock.

There, in the dancing yellow flames, he could see his wife's face. She appeared every bit as enraged as she had two days earlier, the last time the trapper had set eyes on her.

"Making yourself a meal, are you?" the fire-wife shrieked. "Stuffing your face before you make the slightest effort to find me and give me a decent burial! Isn't that just like you!"

The trapper gave a startled cry, dropped his frying pan and his food and scrambled backward away from the haunted fire.

"Squawking like a baby!" sneered his wife. "Like a sniveling little…"

But before she could finish, the trapper poured a dipper of water over her flaming head. The fire sputtered out and the trapper was relieved to find himself alone once more.

The idea of food no longer appealed to him and the hour was growing late.

"Sleep is what I need," the trapper muttered. "A good long rest will banish these terrible hallucinations from my brain." Afraid to build another fire, he wrapped himself in every blanket that he could find and made himself comfortable upon the sagging old mattress. He would have been content enough had it not been for the bitter storm that arose. The wind howled and shrieked, blowing frigid, damp air through the chinks in the logs and carrying with it the screeching voice of the trapper's wife.

"Lazy as an old dog!" she wailed. "Sleeping when you should be trying to *find me!*"

The trapper struggled out of his layered cocoon and clapped his hands over his ears.

"Leave me be," he moaned as he lit a lamp, all the while trying to not look too directly into the match flame. When he set the lamp down on the washstand, though, he did glance into the battered tin water bucket. There, wavering beneath the thin disk of ice on the surface, was a watery vision of his wrathful wife.

"You're wasting time and shirking your duty!" she screeched. "Get out into the woods and *find me!*"

The trapper could stand no more. Realizing that he would never have a moment's peace until he found his wife's remains, he buttoned his coat, laced his boots and trudged out the door into the dark, cold night.

"*Find me…*" the wife's keening floated over the treetops.

The trapper listened carefully and then attempted to follow the sound of the voice that he had tried, for most of his married life, to avoid.

"*Find me...*" she wailed, and he made every effort to, crashing through the dense underbrush in the biting cold. The source of the wife's harping voice was difficult to pinpoint, though. The trapper would walk for a time in one direction, certain that he was growing closer. But then, without warning, the voice would suddenly seem to be coming from a great distance to the left, or to the right, or even from behind him. The trapper spent hours walking through the forest in circles, until he was frightened, desperate and hopelessly lost.

"I can't find you!" he finally cried into the bitter night. His wife did not answer, but a sudden gust of freezing wind rattled the dry branches that hung above his head. It sounded very much like a low, gloating chuckle.

The trapper froze to death before dawn.

It has been many years since then. The area remains wild and remote, although some outdoor enthusiasts do hike in for camping excursions. Few stay longer than a day or two, though, and none make the journey twice. They say that the area is too far from civilization and that the mind can play tricks on a person there.

For often they hear a woman's voice on the wind, calling for someone to find her.

And sometimes they see the wispy specter of a weary, wandering old trapper who is doomed to follow that shrieking voice for all time.

Insomnia

There once was a young woman who got a terrific deal on a second-hand bed at a yard sale. She was extremely pleased with her purchase until she got the thing home, set it up in her bedroom, put on lovely fresh linens and tucked herself in. Then she realized that she had actually paid far too much, for the old four-poster bed was haunted.

She had just turned out the light and found a comfortable position to sleep in when the springs began to move and creak. The woman was lying as still as a stone, but the mattress bounced and sagged, as though someone was rolling around on top of it. There began a sighing sound then, a constant breathy sighing that was interrupted occasionally by a cough or a bit of throat clearing. This carried on throughout the night, except for a few short periods of relative peace.

For three straight nights this continued, until the young woman was exhausted. She decided to visit the house where the yard sale had taken place.

An older woman answered her knock at the door.

"Oh, that would be my husband," she said when the young woman explained the problem. "He suffered terribly from insomnia. Didn't have a decent night's sleep in all the 40 years we were married."

When the young woman asked what could be done, the widow offered a suggestion.

"Try leaving out a little warm milk in a cup," she suggested.

The woman took the advice and left a lovely cup of frothy warm milk on the bedside table that night. But the very minute she crawled beneath the comforter, she knew that the problem had not been solved. The tossing and turning began immediately and was followed by hours of loud annoying noise.

She went back to the widow.

"The milk didn't work," she complained.

"Oh, dear," said the widow. "Well, try reading a bit of a bedtime story then. That used to help him sometimes."

So, the young woman went home and found a lovely story to read. That evening, just before retiring, she sat beside the bed and read aloud. She felt a bit foolish, but was willing to do anything for a decent night's sleep.

Unfortunately, she didn't have one.

All night long, the bedsprings creaked and the

mattress bounced. All night long, the sounds of moaning, groaning, sighing and sniffing kept the young woman wide awake.

The next day she sought out the widow again. Again, the widow drew on her years of marital experience for the solution.

"Sing him a little song," she urged. "Something sweet and soothing, like a lullaby. He always liked that. Said it knocked him right out."

So, the young woman sang. She sang for hours; she sang every soft, gentle song she knew, and then improvised a few others. Still, the ghost tormented her with his wakefulness.

It had come to the point where the young woman could not tolerate any more. Ill-tempered and fatigued, she marched over to the widow's house and issued a demand.

"I can't take this anymore," she said. "I insist that you buy your bed back."

The widow refused to help.

"I can't do it," she said sympathetically. "I already spent the cash, and anyway, I got no place to put the old bed, not since I bought this lovely half-tester. It's an antique, you know, carved outta oak, with a feather mattress that's as soft as a cloud."

The young woman eyed the widow suspiciously.

"Really," she said as she peered at the large dark circles that hung beneath the widow's eyes. "It doesn't look like it's giving you any rest."

"Not a bit," admitted the widow. "It's a real shame. But I bought the thing from the woman down the street, you see."

"Why should that matter?"

"Well, her hubby passed away just last year," explained the widow. "And he used to snore."

A Nip of Courage

Everyone knew that Grandfather drank; it's just that nobody ever talked about it. Especially not in front of Grandmother, who was a dedicated teetotaler. The two grandchildren, Kevin and David, found the consensual silence to be a curious thing. It did require Grandfather to hide his liquor, though, which provided them with hours of amusement.

The boys had amassed a list of the old man's hiding places and regarded adding to the collection as a great game. There was nothing quite so satisfying to either of the boys as being able to announce to the other one that there was a loose board under the stairs or a false bottom in the antique cabinet, and a bottle of cheap whiskey secreted away there. They never touched those bottles, though; they never dared to. At least not until well after Grandfather had died.

By that time Kevin was 18 years old and David had begun college. Although they no longer lived with their parents and their pious, doddering grand-mother, they were occasional weekend visitors. During those weekends, when the dull hum of farm life became too much to bear, they would search out the stashes.

There was seldom much point. Grandfather, who had been well aware of the cancer that took him away little by little, had obviously planned to leave noth-ing much behind. Some bottles had but an ounce or two in them; others were left with scarcely more than boozy vapors. Still, the systematic search provided the young men with something to do in a dreary old house where there was no stereo system and no cable TV.

One bleak Friday night, while their parents were away at a curling bonspiel and their grandmother was watching an old movie she had seen many times but couldn't remember, Kevin and David made a partic-ularly exciting discovery. On the top shelf of the upstairs linen closet, behind a stack of old woolen blankets, was one of Grandfather's bottles. This one was different, though, in that the amber liquid filled it nearly to the top.

"He barely cracked this one," said Kevin.

"Nice of him to leave us a little something," nod-ded David, who went quietly to the kitchen to get two glasses.

One hour and several toasts later, sleep seemed to

be an inviting option. Kevin rinsed the tumblers under the bathroom faucet while David hid the bottle beneath his bed. Then both fellows slurred their "goodnights" and hit their pillows.

Sedated by the whiskey, they fell asleep almost immediately. But they didn't stay asleep for long.

"PUT IT BACK!"

The voice was thundering, fearsome and familiar. Both Kevin and David bolted upright, their eyes wide and their hearts pounding.

"What was that?" each asked the other. But neither one could say. When all had been quiet for several minutes, save for the muffled audio of Grandmother's television, they looked at one another sheepishly.

"Guess I had a little 'drunk dream,' " said David.

"Me, too," added Kevin, although as he lay back down, he wondered about the extreme coincidence of two people having the same nightmare at exactly the same time.

Before he could even close his eyes, he had the answer.

"PUT IT BACK!"

The same roaring command made the young men jump once more. This time, however, there was no question of whether the voice was a fragment of a dream. This time, it was obvious that the voice was coming from the ghost that was hovering in front of their bedroom door.

It was Grandfather. Although it had been years, the

young men would have recognized his drooping mustache and fierce eyes anywhere. They were the eyes that had sometimes made them quake with fear when they were children. But they had been dark then, not misty, gauzy and pale.

"Does he want the bottle back, do you think?" Kevin asked in a shaky voice.

"I'd say," said David. And then, showing the sort of bravery that only exists in war heroes and older brothers, he pulled the bottle from beneath his bed and walked past the shimmering apparition on his way to the linen closet.

After a moment, he returned to the bedroom. Kevin was still sitting wide-eyed in his bed, but the ghost was gone.

"He faded away," explained Kevin.

"That should be the end of that," David pronounced as he crawled back under the covers. But as it happened, it was not.

"PUT IT BACK!" they heard again, the very instant they tried to close their eyes.

When the brothers looked, they saw the phantom of their grandfather glowering down at them again.

"I did put the bottle back," David groused.

"Maybe he means the whiskey inside the bottle," suggested Kevin.

The two looked at each other then, realizing that they had a serious problem. Aside from the whiskey that remained in the linen closet, there was not a drop to be had in the house. Over the months they had exhausted the dribs and drabs that had been stashed in all the other hiding places. And given their grandmother's enthusiasm for temperance, they knew that there wouldn't be anything else around from which to refill their grandfather's bottle.

The specter roared with displeasure as Kevin and David tried to solve the knotty problem. Then, suddenly, with a whoosh of icy air, he vanished. In place of the spirit's great rumblings there was a soft knocking sound.

"Boys?" came a thin, warbling voice on the other side of the bedroom door. "There's such an awful racket going on! Are you alright?"

"Gran!" the brothers whispered simultaneously. David jumped up and opened the door.

The tiny white-haired woman stepped inside the bedroom and hugged her cardigan more tightly to her thin body.

"Chilly in here!" she stated. "Gotta get you boys one of those space heaters. Now, what was the ruckus about? I couldn't hear my program!"

Kevin hemmed and David hawed. They had not had time to think of an appropriate alibi. They might have managed to fashion one on the spot, but the ghost chose to materialize again at that moment.

The luminescent form began to take shape directly in front of Grandmother. Clouds of vapor coalesced into the fierce face and thick body that were so recognizable. Kevin and David held their breath and hoped that their grandmother would not compound their troubles by suffering a coronary.

She did not. In fact, she quite surprised her grandsons with her reaction.

"Oh, go away, Ben," she shooed, waving her frail hand through the misty form. "I haven't time for you now. The boys have something to tell me."

The ghost vanished with a sound that fell somewhere between a low growl and a whimper. The grandmother turned to Kevin and David again, as though nothing untoward had happened.

"Go on, boys," she urged. "Tell me why it's necessary to make so much noise that I can't understand a word coming out of Jimmy Stewart's mouth."

And so they told her. They were so rattled that they forgot themselves and told her the complete truth. As it turned out, it was the best thing they could have done. Grandmother clearly understood, was far from shocked, and was even able to help.

"So you stole a little of Grandad's hooch, eh? Well, that's no problem. Just fill the bottle up with water, boys. He'll never know the difference."

Kevin and David did as their grandmother suggested and the ghost left them in peace for the remainder of the night.

The next morning, as they sat at the breakfast

table nursing mild hangovers and mugs of hot coffee, David dared to raise the subject again.

"How did you know, Gran?" he asked. "About the trick with the water?"

"Oh, sweetheart!" she laughed, sounding like a girl. "I used to do it all the time! Don't get me wrong, now—I frown on drunkenness; you know that." She shook a bony finger at each of her grandsons and added a stern look for emphasis. But when she saw the boys' hangdog expressions, she softened a bit and gave them each a little wink.

"It was just that dealing with a man like your grandfather," she explained, "sometimes required a wee nip of courage."

A Summer Companion

When Carol saw the scene, it reminded her of one of the lovely delicate watercolors they sold in so many of the touristy little galleries in town. It would be titled something simple, like *Girl by Seaside*. But it wasn't a painting, it was real—her pretty daughter, Molly, was wandering along the cliffs that overlooked the ocean, creating a pastel vision that Carol simply had to capture on film.

Not that Carol needed to be terribly inspired in order to whip out her camera. Though she would never have the eye for light and composition that was required of a serious student of photography, she loved to document her life, and her daughter's, in pictures. And during that summer in the quaint old house by the shore, she had become a more avid shutterbug than usual.

There were pictures of Molly swimming and pictures of Molly sleeping. There were pictures of her in each of the swimsuits that had been purchased especially for the two-month vacation, and pictures of her in her bright new sun dresses. The girl was 11 years old and possessed the slight self-consciousness so often found in those caught awkwardly between childhood and adolescence. Sometimes she was exasperated by Carol's ever-present camera.

"Do you have to photograph *everything* I do, Mom?" she would complain.

"Yes, I do," was Carol's usual good-natured reply.

Carol normally was good-natured, patient and understanding when it came to Molly's quirks and moods. She remembered all too well what it was like to be a girl of that age. There was one aspect of her daughter's behavior she didn't understand, though, and the two clashed over it frequently. That day of the watercolor moment, after Carol had zipped her beloved camera into her fanny pack, they clashed again.

Carol had looked up just in time to see that Molly, lost in some girlish daydream, was wandering dangerously close to the edge of the cliff.

"Molly!" Carol had shouted, but the girl seemed not to hear her.

"Molly!" she screamed much more loudly as she ran to catch up. Carol managed to grasp her daughter's wrist only moments before she would likely have lost her footing on the loose sandy soil.

"What were you thinking? Or were you thinking?" she chastised the girl. "You could have gotten yourself killed!"

Molly said nothing, but looked sheepishly at her feet. She had heard similar lectures throughout the summer, after many accidents or near-accidents that Carol attributed to nothing more than lack of attention. Only the day before she had been dressed down for clumsy behavior after tripping on a loose runner and tumbling down the staircase at the beach house.

Though she had no more to show for it than a bruised knee, her mother had been quick to remind her that she might have broken her neck.

Two days after the incident at the cliff, Carol found herself waiting impatiently in line at the one shop in the little resort town that offered same-day photo developing. By the time she reached the counter, 20 minutes had passed. She was running late and not in the mood to chat, but the clerk insisted on keeping her there.

"Just a minute—one minute," the girl with the nose ring had urged. "Darren wants to talk to you."

She disappeared into the back of the store and re-emerged with a pleasant-looking fellow in a white coat. He turned out to be the technician who had developed Carol's pictures.

"Listen, I hope you don't mind me asking," he said, "but I'm curious. How did you create that trick effect with the ghost?"

When Carol responded with a confused expression, Darren opened her photo packet and found the print in question. It was the one showing Molly on the cliffs above the sea.

"See?" he said as he pointed to the picture. "Is that a double exposure or just my imagination?"

Carol looked. The picture showed the idyllic scene that she remembered, with one additional element. Walking beside Molly there appeared to be the shimmering image of another girl. She was a little taller than Molly and wore a long flowing skirt that accentuated that fact. A thick braid hung down the middle of her back. She stood between Molly and the edge of the steep cliff and appeared to be reaching out to the younger girl. Carol felt a little shiver when she noticed that one pale tapering finger seemed to touch her daughter's hand.

To the technician she said, "I don't know how this happened."

The man looked a little bit embarrassed then.

"My imagination ran away, I guess," he shrugged. "It's probably a bit of this cloud that we're seeing here."

Carol had shrugged and nodded along with the man, but secretly she was intrigued. That evening, after Molly had gone up to her bedroom to read, she took out the envelopes containing all the photos that she had taken since the beginning of the summer. She spread them all out on the kitchen table, turned on the bright, overhead light and examined her collection very carefully.

A couple of the pictures proved interesting.

One was iffy; the misty area of the photo could easily have been attributed to a splash of reflected light. But another—a snapshot taken of Molly in the weathered porch swing—showed a definite shadowy shape sitting primly to one side.

Carol tried to be critical. It could have been some trick of the light; she knew that. But it was a trick of the light that created an image that was identical to the one in the picture taken at the cliff. Carol could distinguish the folds of fabric of a long skirt, and even the shape of a braid. She set the two photos side by side and marveled at what she saw in them.

"Oh, Miss Molly," she said quietly to herself. "I think you have a friend." It made Carol feel good to know that at such an impulsive and careless age Molly had a protective spirit watching over her.

In the days that followed, Carol rarely set her camera down. She was so enchanted by the sweet image that had found its way into her photos that she simply could not wait to capture it again. She snapped pictures of every part of the old house, from the dusty attic to the steep staircase and the breezy front porch. And she photographed Molly even more than usual, until the girl couldn't contain her frustration.

"Mother, I'm peeling potatoes!" she groaned when Carol took a picture of her one evening as the two of them prepared dinner. "Do you really need a photo of that?"

Carol had been just about to answer when the pot of water being boiled for the potatoes went crashing to the floor. Molly jumped back barely in time to avoid being badly scalded.

"How many times have I told you!" Carol shrieked. "You have to be careful when you're working with a hot stove! You can't go waving your hands around for the sake of drama!"

"I wasn't!" protested Molly.

"Pardon me if I don't believe you," snapped Carol. "You can't keep your mind on anything these days!"

Molly burst into tears and ran upstairs to her bedroom. Carol stayed behind to mop up the water and fume in privacy. Neither one ended up having any dinner.

The next day brought a truce, but it was an uneasy one. During the week that followed, mother and daughter conversed awkwardly, when they spoke at all, and Molly found some excuse that took her to bed early every night. Carol spent the lonely hours reading and watching television. One dark, rainy evening, she had two new packages of pictures to look through, which she regarded as a welcome change.

Two photos caught her immediate attention— both for reasons that were unsettling.

First Carol noticed the picture she had taken in the kitchen the night the pot of boiling water had spilled. In it, the steam rising from the pot seemed particularly dense and white. Most interesting was the way that the tendrils that curled from beneath the stainless-steel lid appeared for all the world to be in the shape of five distinct tapering fingers.

Something about that bothered Carol. But not as much as did the other photo in question, a picture she had taken of the beach house's steep narrow staircase. When she looked at that picture, she didn't even need to search for the ghost. She was just there, plainly there, sitting on the third step from the top with her legs stretched out and crossed at the ankles. The spirit was looking boldly into the camera for the picture, and something in her translucent expression made Carol shiver.

"Where are you?" she whispered. "Where are you right now?"

Suddenly it felt very important to know that. Carol snapped a fresh roll of film into her camera and began taking pictures throughout the house.

She worked for two hours, carefully documenting every corner, nook and cranny. She took pictures of empty chairs while wondering if they truly were empty. She took pictures of raindrops on the dark windows while thinking that she might later see the image of a teenaged girl's face superimposed there. She quietly opened Molly's bedroom door and took a picture of her sleeping daughter. Finally, she took a straight-on photo of the staircase, where the phantom had already shown herself so clearly.

The next morning, Carol rose well before Molly did. She tiptoed around, getting dressed and making herself a bit of breakfast. Then quietly she locked the door behind her and drove into town. She was at the photo shop before the girl had even had an opportunity to unlock the door.

"More pictures, huh?" said the girl. "You sure do take a lot." Then she told Carol what she wanted to hear, that because she was the first one in the door, she could have her photos in 45 minutes, give or take.

Carol grabbed a cup of coffee and a newspaper. Before the hour had expired, she was back at the counter in the photo shop, paying for her pictures.

She was prickling with impatience before she even got out of the store. Something told her that there would be something very telling in that batch of photos, something that would explain her strange unease. The minute she was seated in her car, she tore open the envelope and began rifling through the pictures.

Most of them showed nothing. But the two that did show something caused Carol to suck her breath in sharply. Suddenly she realized that Molly's spectral friend was no protector. It was she who had pushed the pot, she who had waited on the stairs to grasp an unsuspecting ankle, she who had tried once to lure Carol's daughter off the edge of a cliff.

Carol threw the pile of photos on the passenger seat, not noticing or caring that most of them slid forward and hit the floor mat. Then she turned the key in the ignition, threw the car in gear and sped home. It wasn't until much later that she came to realize how pointless that had been. After all, everything that was in the pictures had already happened.

"Molly!" Carol screamed as she threw open the front door. She heard nothing but the ringing of her own voice.

"Molly, answer me!" she begged as she ran frantically up the stairs. But there was no answer.

When Carol burst into her daughter's bedroom, it took only a moment to realize that Molly would not be answering her ever again. The girl lay cold, still and slightly blue against the backdrop of snowy linen. Encircling her small throat was a necklace of deep purple bruises. Molly was dead, Molly had been strangled, and Carol had known it since the moment she had raced away from the photo shop. She had known because she had seen it in two of the photos.

The one she had taken of her sleeping daughter the night before showed the ghost's gauzy form hovering over the bed. Her slender white hands had been gripping the girl's neck. The specter's eyes had been on the camera, though, and her expression was smug and vile. As horrifying as that was, the second photo had been worse. It was the second photo that was destined to haunt Carol until the end of her days.

It was a picture of the staircase. On one of the steps sat the ghost, looking loathsome and pleased all at once. Pleased, no doubt, because she was no longer alone. Her vaporous white arm was draped possessively around the shoulder of an equally transparent phantom companion. The companion looked confused and frightened, and was as insubstantial as a cloud—but her face was instantly recognizable to Carol. It was a face that she had looked into a million times and photographed probably a thousand.

It was her daughter who was the second spectral figure in the photograph.

It was Molly.

Frosty

"Gimme a newspaper and a lemon-lime frosty."

Carrie collected the coins that the man had tossed on the counter and set them on the cash register. She slid a newspaper across the clear glass surface that allowed people to choose from a variety of colorful scratch-and-win lottery tickets. Then she set a plastic cup on the sticky metal tray of the frosty machine and pulled the cracked, plastic handle. As gobs of sickly-green slush plopped into the cup, she was reminded, for the 15th time that morning, how much she hated her summer job.

Carrie hated having to be at the convenience store at seven o'clock in the morning when she worked the early shift. She equally hated having to stay until midnight on the late shift. She hated the rude customers and the kids who shoplifted, and the people who thought that she had all the time in the world to chat. She hated making coffee, cleaning graffiti off the bathroom walls and having to mop the dull tile floor with the old ragged mop and rolling bucket with its wonky, squeaky wheels. She hated the buzzer over the door and the finicky "no sale" button on the cash register. Most of all, though, more than anything else, Carrie hated the huge, grumbling metal machine with the sign that read "FROST KING."

The Frost King would occasionally leak, slowly spreading pools of syrup that attracted flies. It also made noises—chugging, groaning, on-its-last-mechanical-legs sorts of noises, ranging in intensity from annoying to concerning. Once, after pouring a strawberry frosty that had actually caused the cold metal beast to violently shudder, Carrie had suggested to the store's owner that it was time to invest in a new machine.

"You kids don't know anything about money, except to spend, spend, spend!" he had lectured. "Ain't nothin' wrong with Frosty Frank. You just gotta know how to coax him along."

Frosty Frank. Carrie knew that once people had named their appliances, they weren't likely to trade up until the unit in question was really good and dead. So she did her best to "coax the machine along" and never raised the subject again.

Not that she hadn't been tempted to. Especially once she began to suspect that the gear-gnashing, syrup-dripping Frost King was haunted.

"I think it's evil," she once told a friend, who told Carrie, in turn, that she was crazy. But the friend didn't know how the hulking contraption would sometimes wheeze and vibrate when Carrie walked past it. And no one knew that it had bitten her.

She had been pouring out a rarely requested blueberry frosty when it happened. There was a trick to stopping the machine at just the right moment—when the cup would be full but not overflowing down the side—and it required a deft movement of the handle. Carrie performed the maneuver a little too quickly, though, and managed to pinch her finger in the crack that ran the length of the plastic handle. When she jerked her hand away, the jagged edge of the broken plastic sliced open the pad of her fingertip. A few drops of blood fell into the machine's runoff tray.

"You better not be bleeding in my frosty," the teenaged customer who had been counting out his nickels and dimes complained.

"Don't worry," Carrie replied. "It won't cost you any extra."

From that day forward, she was certain that the Frost King was watching her. Sometimes the sensation of eyes upon her would be so strong that she would turn from whatever she was doing, sure that a customer was waiting to catch her attention. Usually there was no one there. All Carrie would see was her own warped image reflected in one of the bent tin panels of the despised machine.

It made more unexplainable noises after the accident, too. The gurgling, churning and grinding began to happen at any time, and not only when a drink had just been poured. Once, when Carrie slipped and fell while mopping the floor, old Frosty emitted what sounded very much like a low, guttural chuckle.

At the beginning of the summer, Carrie thought that the machine was messy, loud and annoyingly difficult to operate. By mid-August, she thought that it was vindictive, predatory and probably possessed. One quiet weeknight, while working a long evening shift, she decided that it was entirely too creepy to deal with.

"Take that, Frost King," she said as she draped a large cloth over the front of the unit. "You've been dethroned." She wrote "out of order" on a large piece of cardboard, folded it in half and placed it on top of the machine. Then she turned her back to it and busied herself with some paperwork beside the cash register.

Several minutes later there was a wrenching sound. Carrie stopped what she was doing and remained perfectly still, waiting to see if she would hear the strange noise again. She did, and before she could turn to see what was the cause of it, something small rolled into the scuffed toe of her sneaker. It was one of the rusted bolts that was supposed to hold the Frost King's metal legs securely to the floor.

Carrie kicked it back beneath the machine.

"So, you shook yourself loose, huh?" she said to the silent King. "I think I'll have to report you as a safety hazard." Then, because she was a little nervous and because she felt that she had enough of an excuse, Carrie reached around back of the unit and pulled its thick black power cord out of the outlet. A burbling sort of liquid growl issued from the bowels of the machine.

"Try throwing your battered body parts at me *now*, you rotting heap," she said. Then, feeling victorious, she went off to the back of the store to restock the cooler.

When Carrie re-emerged from the storeroom a few minutes later, the first thing that she saw was the Frost King. That was odd, because normally the beast couldn't be seen from the rear door marked "Employees Only." Had it been in its usual position, it would have been hidden from Carrie's view by the potato chip rack. But it wasn't hidden; it was in plain sight, and that told her that the thing had moved.

She walked to the front of the store, but stayed deliberately on the customers' side of the counter. From there she could see everything that she needed to see—like the scarred patches on the tile where each metal leg had spent a decade gouging out its home, and the dark pool of strawberry syrup that had oozed from the very bottom of the machine but was now, somehow, off to the side of it. She could see the black electrical cord too, and how obvious it was that it would not be possible to stretch it as far as the outlet from the position it was in.

The Frost King had moved. The Frost King was after her.

Carrie ran for the front door and threw it open with such force that she snapped the wire connected to the annoying buzzer.

It was a cold, drizzly night. After a while, Carrie wasn't sure if she was shivering from the cold or from fear. She just knew that she wasn't quite ready to leave the safety of the parking lot in order to retrieve her jacket from inside the store. She needed to take some more deep breaths of cold, damp air and try to clear her head.

As she was doing that, a car pulled into the parking lot. It rolled to a stop directly in front of the store and the headlights faded to black. A tall, skinny man, the first customer in 90 minutes, jumped out of the vehicle. As he headed for the doors, he looked at Carrie and rapped his knuckles sharply on the hood of his car.

"Hey, counter girl!" he snapped. "Break's over! I need a pack of smokes!"

Carrie hesitantly followed the rude man inside the store. She told herself that the evil machine couldn't do anything in front of a witness. Then she promised herself that the instant the man was gone she would phone her boss and swear that she was too sick to work for another minute. Still, she found it difficult to actually walk around to the service side of the counter.

The customer stated his brand and slapped his money on the counter.

"Hurry it up," he complained when Carrie took a minute getting to the cash register. The instant she handed him his change, he was gone. Carrie was uneasy about being alone in the store again, but was relieved that she could go into the back to make her phone call.

Before she could take a single step in that direction, though, something whipped around her ankles and pulled tight, lashing her legs together. Carrie let out a shocked little scream and looked down to see that she had been hog-tied by the Frost King's power cord. Before she could do a thing, the cord yanked her feet out from under her. Carrie went crashing to the hard tile floor. On the way down, her head hit the register and sent the cash drawer springing out.

She couldn't get her eyes to focus properly after that, and she couldn't stand up. Still, she made a brave, if lame, attempt to crawl to the door and escape. The thick black cord wouldn't let her, though. It dragged her back behind the counter, then looped around her left wrist and yanked hard, flipping her over onto her back. Carrie felt the floor tremble slightly beneath her body. She watched the blurred, double image of her handmade "out of order" sign as it tumbled from its perch and landed squarely on her chest.

The last sound Carrie heard was the Frost King grinding to life. The last thing she felt was the first wet, freezing splatter of slush landing on her face.

❦ ❦ ❦

Later everyone said that it was such a senseless sort of thing, since the robber didn't even end up emptying the cash drawer. Of course there was plenty of speculation that the incident hadn't been about robbery at all, but rather about committing a cruel and sadistic murder. Carrie's body had been found in a puddle of melting ice and sticky syrup. She was bloated full of frozen slush.

It was sort of ironic, they said, that the coroner had to wait two full days before the girl's innards had thawed out to the degree that an autopsy could be performed.

Ironic because the cause of death was ruled to be extreme hypothermia.

Carrie had been decidedly frosty.

The East Elevator

Mrs. Posey pushed the button for the 17th floor and the elevator doors were sliding shut. She was a little surprised when a tall man in a black suit stepped through the gap at the very last second to join her in the car.

It was a pleasant surprise. Although there were easily 200 people living in Mrs. Posey's large high-rise apartment building, she rarely saw any of them. People tended to stay locked behind their doors. So Mrs. Posey, who was elderly and lonely, welcomed any opportunity for a bit of a social visit. Even if it only lasted the duration of an elevator ride.

"Oh, the 12th floor!" she remarked when the tall man pushed the button. "The lady who runs the convenience store downstairs used to live on the 12th floor, you know. But then she bought a condominium in that new development down the block."

The man said nothing. He didn't turn to greet Mrs. Posey with a smile or a nod, and he did nothing to acknowledge that she had spoken to him. He simply stared straight ahead, his hands clasped in front of him, his pale features arranged in a somber expression.

A lesser woman might have been put off. But Mrs. Posey was determined to have a conversation.

"It's nice to have a bit of company for the ride upstairs," she said. "Most of the tenants these days take the elevator by the west door. But I like this one, on account of it's closer to my apartment."

The man did nothing and said nothing. He stared blankly ahead at the dull metallic finish of the elevator doors.

Mrs. Posey decided to take a different approach. She would ask the man a direct question, which would force him to respond.

"Do you live here yourself, or are you visiting someone?" she inquired.

Still, the man said nothing. Then the number 12 lit up on the bank of buttons, and the elevator car shuddered to a stop. The door slid open and the tall, thin fellow with the dark suit and mood to match stepped out of the elevator onto the patterned carpet of the hall.

His departure left Mrs. Posey with a certain odd feeling, a certain disconnectedness. It made her recall a conversation she had once overheard in the lobby. One woman had been whispering to another that there was a ghost in the building, a ghost that haunted the east elevator.

Mrs. Posey felt a little chill as she looked out at the dark man with the vacant stare. As the elevator doors slid shut, she sincerely wondered if she had just met the ghost.

❧ ❧ ❧

When the elevator doors closed behind him, Timothy Kent felt a huge surge of relief. He decided then and there that he would only use the west elevator from that day forward.

His neighbor had told him to avoid the east elevator; he had said that it was haunted. But Tim Kent had laughed at the time. He wasn't the sort to believe in such fanciful things.

Of course that was before he had ridden for 12 floors all alone with a mysterious column of shimmering, ice-cold air.

The Double

There were certain times in Mona Howard's life when she felt as though she was constantly looking into a mirror. It was nothing to do with vanity, though; it was because of the doppelganger that had haunted her for all of her days.

In Mona's first memory of the ghostly double, she was no more than four; still a baby, really, with blond pigtails and scabby knees. She had been playing with her tea set when another little girl appeared. The other little girl looked exactly like her. She could do entertaining things that Mona couldn't do, though, like drift across the nursery floor without actually moving her feet. And she could vanish in a flash whenever another person came into the room. The little girl who looked just like Mona was obviously shy around adults, so Mona decided that it would be kind to keep her existence a secret.

By the time Mona was old enough to realize that her double was not a real girl at all, she was also wise enough to understand that most people were uncomfortable knowing about such things. So she remained secretive. There were many days when she would spot the face full of freckles just like her own across a crowded classroom. And there were many nights when she would awaken to see that her extra pillow was covered with a spill of familiar sandy-colored tresses. But Mona always kept these things to herself. There was no sense in upsetting anyone over something so benign.

When she was a teenager, she began to see a certain pattern to the ghostly visits. On the evening before an important exam, her double was guaranteed to appear. She would hover about, smiling encouragingly while Mona studied. The doppelganger was also sure to visit when Mona had been fighting with her best friend or had been dumped by a boy. Heartbreak and stress always brought Mona face-to-face with the comforting, supportive version of her own image.

On occasion, the ghost would surprise her or confuse her. When Mona had been a new college graduate on the way to her first-ever job interview, she turned a

202 Campfire Ghost Stories

corner and had to stop short to avoid crashing into a mirror. As she regained her balance, she realized that there was no mirrored surface. It was the spirit, dressed in an identical new navy suit, with her hair twisted into an identical French braid. The image faded away after a moment, but Mona was left with a sense of confidence and well-being. She continued on to her interview and came away with a good job.

Mona's spirit double was there with her when she was a bride and when she had each of her two children. When she suffered from bouts of sleeplessness, the spirit often appeared at some point as she sat up through the night. When Mona was in the midst of a challenging day, it was never a surprise for her to glance up and see an identically tall woman with identical lines around her eyes and identical gray streaks at her temples. Sometimes the ghost would linger quietly for half an hour and sometimes Mona would only catch a fleeting image. Always, though, there would be the lingering impression of comfort.

All through her life, Mona had accepted the presence of her doppelganger. She had come to rely on the spirit and draw strength from it. What she hadn't done, ever, was tell anyone about it. And she never planned to. But that plan changed on the day she spent at the bedside of her dying mother.

Mona had been keeping her mother company for hours when she decided to go down to the hospital cafeteria to buy a sandwich and a cup of coffee. When she came back 10 minutes later, her mother was shaking her head in wonder.

"I saw the most amazing thing," she said in the dry whisper that had become her regular speaking voice. "When you rose from your chair to leave the room, Mona, it was like you divided into two people. One of you walked away and the other stayed here in the chair watching over me. Then, just a few seconds before you returned, the other image of you faded away. It was remarkable."

Mona looked into her mother's pale, thin face. She knew that her life was quickly slipping away. Mona recognized her last chance to share her lifetime secret with her mother and she took it.

She spoke at length, telling her mother about the ghost that had looked exactly like her all through her life. She described the silent camaraderie, the feeling of support and the lasting comfort that had always accompanied the visits.

"There's not a thing that's bad about it," Mona stressed. "It's just the one thing that I never told you."

Mona's mother nodded and with great effort reached over to take her daughter's hand.

"Then, in turn, I should share the one thing I never told you," she whispered.

Mona leaned in closely to listen.

"You had an identical twin sister, darling," Mona's mother said gently. *"A twin sister who died at birth."*

Your Fortune — Five Dollars

Everyone who lived in the little prairie town agreed: July was the best month of the year. Most also agreed on the reason: in July the carnival came to town—and *everybody* loved the carnival.

For three days the dusty parcel of land by the local arena was turned into a magically gaudy Shangri-la. Enormous, dangerous-looking rides were assembled alongside food stands that sold the most tempting combinations of sugar, lard and salt. There were games of chance—although whether anyone actually had a chance of winning was subject for debate—and there was always a fun house, where a person could get lost amidst their own bizarre reflections in a maze of distorted mirrors. Best of all, there was Madam Zora, the old gypsy who spent her days in a sweltering little tent where the sign outside always read "Your Fortune—Five Dollars."

There were some people who swore by Madam Zora's accuracy. They said that she was the real deal, one of the best, able to tell you anything that you wanted to know about either your future or your past. Of course an uptight few claimed that fortune-telling was the devil's business, and many skeptics said that it was all nonsense. But even those non-believers would generally admit that it was highly entertaining non-sense, and that for five dollars you couldn't really go

wrong. For the most part, the only complaint you would hear about Madam Zora was that she was only available for those three short days out of the year. Aside from that, everyone thought that she was terrific.

Well, almost everyone. There were the aforementioned religious zealots, and there was Thelma Patterson. It was widely known that Thelma was dissatisfied with the predictions and advice that the old gypsy had given her.

It all started one July when Thelma went to Madam Zora with a specific request.

"I want to start a business," she said. "Something where I can be my own boss and make a lot of money. I know I've got the gumption, but I need an idea."

Zora nodded in her wise way and stared deeply into her mysterious crystal ball.

"Yes, yes," she intoned. "I envision great success. You will do something from your home—something that involves sewing. You will make a great name for yourself as a seamstress of dramatic fashions."

Thelma went home brimming with excitement and was ready to map out a business plan. That year, she put all her energy into designing sweeping dresses and caftans and all manner of wild, flowing garments. She discovered that no one really shared her taste for the over-the-top style, however, and the venture failed.

The following July, she was fuming as she stood in line to see Madam Zora.

"Your prediction sucked," Thelma announced when she finally entered the stuffy little tent. "The dressmaking thing didn't work out at all." Still, she was willing to slide another five-dollar bill across the faded tablecloth and let Madam Zora take a second shot.

"I still see success to come," the gypsy promised. "I see much money and vivid colors on your lips and eyes." It was determined on that visit that Thelma was destined to make her fortune selling cosmetics door-to-door.

Once again, Thelma threw herself into her project. She invested in a huge pink case of makeup and studied books and instructional videos so that she could offer professional advice on how to apply it. Then she dressed up and walked all over town with her newly acquired products and skills.

No one was interested. The women of the town seemed to be happy with the 99-cent lipsticks and eye shadows that they could buy at the drugstore. They weren't prepared to accept beauty advice from the likes of someone as odd as Thelma Patterson. In the end, she was left with a pile of unsold cosmetics and a broken dream.

Thelma was determined to have a word with the person responsible for breaking that dream.

"Twice before I've come to you for help and twice you've given me bad advice!" she raged at Madam Zora on her third visit to the carnival. "I'm going to tell everyone in town that you're nothing but a con artist!"

The fortune-teller was confused and flustered. She took pride in her predictions and rarely received a complaint.

"Wait," she begged in her strange thick accent. "Let me look into the future for you one more time."

Thelma reluctantly sat down across from the gypsy, who peered into the crystal with great intensity.

"I swear to you, this is what the spirits say," the old woman muttered. "You will be in a successful business by the end of the day. What it is, I do not know. But your success—I would bet my crystal ball on it."

Thelma snorted in disbelief.

"You're a fraud," she hissed as she rose from her chair. When she turned to storm dramatically out of the dimly lit tent, however, she caught her toe on the edge of Madam Zora's frayed old Persian rug. She fell down hard enough to break her leg, which made it rather apparent that she wouldn't be entering into any successful business ventures on that particular day.

And so, because she was a gypsy of her word, Madam Zora left town without her beloved crystal ball.

When the venerable fortune-teller returned to the same town the next year, she noticed that business had fallen off dramatically. There were the usual crowds looking to ride the creaky Ferris wheel, play the crooked games and eat big helpings of corn dogs and fried dough—but those people were no longer lining up outside of her dingy tent to find out what the future held in store. It was confusing, to say the least.

Had Madam Zora looked into her new crystal ball for an explanation, it might have shown her Thelma Patterson.

The crystal would have shown not the old Thelma, but a reinvented one—dramatically made-up, sporting long red fingernails and huge pieces of costume jewelry. It would have shown her happily seated in front of Madam Zora's old crystal ball, wearing a flowing caftan of her own design, in a richly colored fabric of some dramatic celestial pattern.

The crystal might also have shown Madam Zora that outside Thelma's front door was a year-old hand-painted sign with a somewhat familiar message.

In scripted letters large enough to be seen all the way to the front street, where the line-ups sometimes extended, it read:

"Your Fortune—Ten Dollars."

The Caretaker

The quaint little house that had the "for rent" sign on the front lawn was so charming, so absolutely inviting, that Jeannie and Peter were forced to stop and have a closer look. After writing down the phone number and address of the property management company, they followed the curved path to the front door. The place appeared to be empty and the young couple saw no harm in snooping around a bit.

The half-moon window at the entrance was too high for Jeannie to reach, but on tiptoe Peter found that he was able to peer through it. He had been describing what he was seeing—gleaming, bare hardwood floors and a lovely archway between the living and dining area—when he was shocked nearly out of his wits. One moment he had been looking at an empty room. The next, a chalky white face appeared just inches away from his own on the opposite side of the glass.

Much to his embarrassment, Peter gave an involuntary little shriek. He jumped back from the door so quickly that he nearly lost his balance and fell.

"What...?" asked Jeannie. It was all that she had time to say, for the door opened almost immediately. Standing on the opposite side of the sill was a smiling, white-haired matron.

"Oh, I gave you a fright! I am so sorry!" she said to Peter. "It's just that I wasn't expecting anyone and I didn't hear you knock."

"Well, I'm afraid we didn't," Peter replied in an embarrassed tone. "I apologize for peeking through the window like that, but we were under the impression that the house was vacant."

"We're looking for a nice house like this to rent," Jeannie explained.

"Of course! Of course! Come in and look around!" the woman said. She opened the door wider and took a step back, allowing the young couple to pass over the threshold.

"Have you been married long?" she asked as she closed the door behind them.

Jeannie thought it to be an odd question coming from someone they had only just met.

"A few weeks," she said. "Why do you ask?"

"Oh, no reason," the woman laughed. "I guess I'm just a little old-fashioned. One never knows these days if a couple is married or simply 'together,' isn't that right? Come, come; feel free to walk about. This is the parlor. The 'living room,' I suppose you'd call it."

Peter and Jeannie took a self-conscious little tour of the living room. It was bright and spacious, with a high coved ceiling.

"My piano would fit in here," Jeannie commented.

The white-haired woman appeared delighted.

"Oh, do you play?" she asked. "I used to play, such a very long time ago. But then my piano was sold. I've often thought that, given the chance, I'd like to take it up again."

The woman drifted off to the next room then, without indicating whether her guests were expected to follow. Peter and Jeannie looked at one another questioningly.

"Should we?" Jeannie mouthed silently.

Peter shrugged, "Why not?" The couple followed the hollow sound of the woman's sensible shoes.

"Do you do much baking?" the woman asked when all three had gathered in the sunny kitchen. "I think you'll find that there's plenty of good counter space for rolling out dough."

"Well," said Jeannie, "if it can't be zapped in the microwave, I'm hopeless."

"Microwave?" the woman asked vaguely and glanced around the kitchen.

Peter noticed that the range and refrigerator were the only appliances.

"Don't worry," he said. "We have our own. Couldn't live without it."

The woman nodded and smiled and pointed to the view outside the large kitchen windows.

"The garden," she explained. "It's very handy, I think, to have it right outside the kitchen door. Will you keep it up?"

"I beg your pardon?" Jeannie and Peter each said.

"Will you keep up the garden?" the woman patiently repeated. "It would be such a waste if it were to become overgrown and wild, don't you agree?"

Jeannie realized then that the woman was not simply making small talk. Clearly there were right and wrong answers to the chatty questions she was asking. Clearly she and Peter were in the process of being interviewed as potential tenants.

"Well," she said and cleared her throat, "I've never tended that large a vegetable patch before, but I think I could manage it. I have a bit of a green thumb."

The white-haired woman seemed pleased.

"Well, that's fine. I always say 'try your best—that's the most anyone can ask of you.'"

She turned and walked briskly down the back hall toward the staircase.

"Come along," she said as she beckoned Jeannie and Peter to follow her, "you must see the upstairs."

Peter grabbed his wife's arm and held her back a little.

"A green thumb?" he mocked her in a low voice. "Only if you dipped it in paint, honey."

"Shhhh!" Jeannie hissed as she shot Peter a dark look of warning. "I love this house. I *want* this house. And I think we're in the application process right now!"

She pulled away then and ran lightly up the stairs behind their guide.

"What lovely wallpaper!" Peter could hear her cooing from the second-floor landing. He laughed at his wife's obvious fawning, but was careful to do so quietly. Though he was less inclined to audition for the woman's approval, Peter had to admit that he liked the house too.

When he caught up with the two women, they were touring the master bedroom.

"No closet space. Something should have been done about that long ago." The white-haired woman clucked her tongue in disapproval.

Jeannie nodded in agreement.

"A nice wardrobe would solve that problem, though," she suggested. "Something in this corner, say? My parents have one that they don't use anymore."

The woman raised an approving eyebrow.

"That would do the trick," she said. "That would serve nicely without any horrible renovating. I hate plaster dust and all the noise of power tools! Oh!" The woman clapped her hands over her ears in exasperation and walked off in the direction of the second bedroom. Peter and Jeannie avoided each other's eyes, for fear of laughing.

The second bedroom was smaller than the master but more charming. There was a dormer with a window seat and a lovely view of the backyard. Jeannie gasped with pleasure when she walked through the door.

"Oh, Peter!" she said. "Wouldn't this make a lovely nursery?"

Peter was about to comment, but the woman spoke first.

"It has in the past," she said. "Let me show you."

She opened the closet door and pointed at the highest shelf.

"Say, could you?" she motioned for Peter to come over. "I can't begin to reach that. Feel around on the top shelf there and you'll find something interesting."

Peter obediently ran his hand along the dusty shelf. After a moment, his fingers touched something.

"It's a toy," he said as he took the item down. "A little wooden truck."

"Handmade," the white-haired woman pronounced. "You just can't find that kind of craftsmanship anymore. No one has the time for quality." She fluttered her hands in the air as if to dismiss the unpleasant thought as she left the room.

In the time that it took the trio to descend the staircase, the woman managed to make several more thinly disguised inquiries.

"I don't know that you could entertain on much of a scale in this house...do you enjoy large, boisterous parties?"

"Occasionally there is some small repair to take care of...but you look like a handy sort of fellow."

"The hardwood squeaks a little, but that adds

character, don't you think? I can't imagine covering it over with some horrid carpeting."

Peter and Jeannie made their replies and what they said seemed to please the woman. When they arrived back at the front foyer, she turned to them and smiled.

"Tell me," she said, "do you like the house? I mean, do you *really, truly* like it?"

"Oh, yes," breathed Jeannie. "Very much."

Peter nodded and mumbled in the affirmative.

"Good," said the woman in an intensely serious tone, "because I feel that you are very well-suited to it. Very well-suited, indeed. I would urge you to go directly to the property managers and make a deposit before anyone else can."

Peter and Jeannie looked confused.

"Aren't *you* with the property management company?" Peter asked.

The woman smiled and shook her tidily coifed gray head.

"I'm more of a caretaker," she explained. "I look in on the place. I used to live here actually, a long time ago."

She told them to hurry along and shooed them out the front door. Before either Peter or Jeannie could thank the woman for the impromptu tour, they found themselves back on the porch.

"Goodbye…" Jeannie turned to say, but the door had already been closed.

Peter looked at his wife and arched one eyebrow.

"Bit of an odd duck," he said.

Jeannie nodded in agreement, but wasn't about to waste time analyzing the strange woman's behavior.

"It's four thirty," she said. "The property management firm probably doesn't close until five. If we hurry, we can make it."

They did hurry and they did make it. By the end of the afternoon, they had filled out the required forms and put down a deposit on the charming little house with the garden and the perfect nursery.

There was some confusion when they mentioned meeting the caretaker. But it didn't seem to be a huge issue.

"Lotta people work here," the man with the application forms had said. "I don't know the half of 'em or what they do."

It was a curious thing but a forgettable one, particularly amidst the excitement of finding the ideal house. Peter and Jeannie didn't mention the strange woman again, even to each other, until the day they moved in.

They were standing at the front door, juggling the first of many boxes and their new house keys. As they stood there, Peter was reminded of the day they found the house, when he stood on his toes in order to peek through the half-moon window.

"Jeannie," he said, "how tall would you say that

woman was? The caretaker who gave us the third degree?"

Jeannie set down the box she was carrying and let her breath out with a *whoosh*.

"Oh, I don't know," she said. "Five-two, maybe? Five-three? Not tall. She couldn't reach the top shelf of the bedroom closet, remember? Why do you ask?"

Peter had a moment of total recall then, a vivid memory of the woman's pale face appearing directly in front of his own on the opposite side of the glass. It was enough to make the hairs on his arms stand at high alert.

But he forced a casual smile for his wife.

"No reason," he said.

Jeannie turned the shiny new key in the lock and the door opened wide. Then the young couple, who were married and promised to tend the garden, who hoped to use the second bedroom as a nursery and didn't care for loud parties, walked into the house to which they were so well-suited.

Only one of them was wondering when the ghostly piano music would begin.

Afterword
One More Story

The day had been filled with canoeing and hiking. The kids who sat around the fire pit were sunburned and spent. Still, they were unwilling to end the magical evening—the time when they could sit beneath the stars, pull molten marshmallows from the pared tips of crooked sticks and listen to the night sounds of the forest.

"Tell us one more story," they begged their leader, although many of them were yawning and the fire had burned down to a circle of glowing embers.

"Tell us something else that's scary," requested one wide-eyed kid who couldn't stop scratching his mosquito bites.

"Or something that has magic in it," suggested a tall, freckled girl.

But the group leader, who had been sitting all evening on a broad flat tree stump, refused.

"I've told you all the stories I know," he said as he stood up and stretched his tired limbs. "Well, all except one. And you don't want to hear that one."

"*We do!*" the campers cried all together. "*We do want to hear it!*"

But the leader would only smile and firmly shake his head.

"Let's collect all our trash before we turn in," he said to the group.

The kids groaned their complaints but did as they were told. They wandered around the campsite collecting empty potato-chip bags, soda cans and other things that did not belong scattered about in the wilds. As they went about their chore, though, they grew increasingly curious and tried to guess what the secret story might be.

One of the kids looked at the leader and noticed the way that his long shaggy hair hung over his ears.

"Is it a werewolf story?" he asked.

A girl who wore her hair in one long coppery braid that hung down her back thought that the leader had been looking pale—likely because he had slept for so much of the day.

"Is it a vampire story?" she wondered aloud.

The youngest child in the group had for days been speculating about what the leader kept in the strange-looking charm that hung from a chain around his neck. He wanted to ask him about it, but felt too foolish.

"Is it a witch story?" the boy asked instead.

A tall, young fellow who had been sitting directly opposite the leader all evening and had watched the heat waves from the fire turn his features into a shimmering, insubstantial vision, had another theory.

"I bet it's a story about a ghost," he guessed.

As the leader walked past a girl with blond curls

and tiny rimless spectacles, she heard that his canvas shoes were still squishing with lake water.

"I bet it's about a creature from the deep," she mused.

One of the older boys, who had a definite taste for the more frightening tales, looked up at the leader and thought he saw a strange, wild glint in the man's eyes.

"I bet it's a story about an ax-wielding maniac," he said.

The leader continued to shake his head as he collected everyone's contributions of trash in an airtight container.

"You're all wrong," he said as he packed the garbage down.

"But why can't you tell us?" the kids whined collectively. "We want to hear it!"

"No, you *don't*," the leader stressed as he turned away from them and picked up the lid for the container. "Trust me when I tell you that you *don't* want to hear this story."

The leader's voice had begun to sound a little strange, a little lower than usual. He was shivering slightly, and the muscles of his shoulders were tensing beneath the thin fabric of his T-shirt. He kept his back to the group and spent a long time fastening the lid of the container. None of the kids really noticed. They were all much too intent upon the idea of the forbidden story.

"*Why don't we want to hear it?*" the group demanded.

The leader stood up straight then, stretching out his back and lifting his head. He seemed taller than he had only minutes before. As he turned to face the campers ever so slowly, the reason became apparent.

He had transformed.

The leader had transformed into something that was loathsome beyond description, horrifying beyond anything that they had ever created in their childish imaginations.

"*You don't want to hear it,*" he gurgled in a voice that had become choked, guttural and monstrous, "*because there's no telling how it ends!*"

The leader spread open his massive jaws then, raised up what had once been his hands, and advanced upon the group.

The screams carried far over the treetops and into the lonely wilderness.

And then there was darkness as the remains of the fire died out.

The End

GHOST
HOUSE

Ghost House Books

Look for these volumes in our popular ghost story series:

Canadian Ghost Stories	1-55105-302-0
Even More Ghost Stories of Alberta	1-55105-323-3
Ghost Stories of California	1-55105-237-7
Ghost Stories of Hollywood	1-55105-241-5
Ghost Stories of Texas	1-55105-330-6
Ghost Stories of the Rocky Mountains	1-55105-165-6
Ghosts, Werewolves, Witches and Vampires	1-55105-333-0
More Ghost Stories of Saskatchewan	1-55105-276-8
Ontario Ghost Stories, Vol. I	1-55105-203-2

Coming soon...

Watch for these upcoming volumes from Ghost House Books:

Haunted Theaters	1-894877-04-7
Ghost Stories of Indiana	1-894877-06-3
Ghost Stories of Michigan	1-894877-05-5
Ghost Stories of the Maritimes, Vol. II	1-894877-01-2
A Haunted Country Christmas	1-894877-15-2
Haunted Hotels	1-894877-03-9
Ontario Ghost Stories, Vol. II	1-894877-14-4

Available from your local bookseller.

For more information, contact our customer service department. In the
United States, call 1-800-518-3541. In Canada, call 1-800-661-9017.